From This Text

A Fifty-Two-Week Bible Study
Focused on Faith

Beverly A. Johnson

From This Text – A Fifty-Two-Week Bible Study Focused on Faith

CrossLink Publishing
www.crosslink.org

Copyright, © 2013 Beverly A. Johnson
All rights reserved. No part of this book may be reproduced in any form, except for brief quotations in reviews, without the written permission of the author.

Printed in the United States of America. All rights reserved under International Copyright Law.

ISBN 978-1-936746-67-5
Library of Congress Control Number: 2013946386

Scriptural quotations marked NIV® are taken from the Holy Bible, NEW INTERNATIONAL VERSION®. Copyright © 1973, 1978, 1984, 2011 by Biblica, Inc. Used by permission. All rights reserved worldwide.

Scripture quotations marked KJV are taken from the King James Version of the Bible.

To my grandsons, Damien and JaShon. Always remember that Granny loves you, but God loves you more.

Acknowledgments

This book has been the result of a ten-year spiritual and physical struggle. Thank God that Satan has not prevailed in either battle. It is impossible to thank every preacher who has inspired me. I will have to start by thanking Reverend Madison Clark Jr. of the Good Hope Baptist Church, Westlake, Louisiana, for his support when I began to write and speak so many years ago.

Special thanks to Dr. C. W. Wallace, Pastor of Pilgrim Rest Missionary Baptist Church, Dallas, Texas, for his inspirational sermons and teachings during this ten-year struggle.

I will always be grateful to the Adult II Sunday School class at Pilgrim Rest, who listened to me what seemed like every Sunday morning as I shared with them as the Holy Spirit blessed me with inspirational thoughts.

Thanks to Mrs. Linda Parsons, who read the draft of the book and shared her positive thoughts with me when I really needed to hear them.

Thanks to everyone who agreed to contribute their reviews. I am thankful for the support of my husband, Carl and my children, Kevin and Tiffanie.

Special thanks to Reverend Alvin J. Noel for his wonderful Foreword.

I could not mention everyone by name. However, to all my family and friends, please know that your love, prayers, and support mean so much to me and I thank God for you all.

Contents

Foreword

Capturing our attention with the title *From This Text* to the development of each Christian attribute, the author reinforces the importance of being receptive to God's word, of initiating a "Spirit-inspired" study of God's word, and of implementing God's word. We read God's word for inspiration, we study for information, and we live because of transformation.

God wants us to acquire each attribute described in the chapter headings of the book. After reviewing the chapters, I was concerned that Love was not listed as one of the chapter headings. However, after considering the chapter headings of Character, Forgiveness, Trust, Courage, Perseverance, Faith, Humility, Power, Obedience, Intercessory Prayer, Miracles, Sound Decision Making, and Preparation, I have determined that all the arrows pointed toward Jesus. And, of course, Jesus is Love.

I would like to suggest that, while there are some things that we don't want to leave behind, there are certainly some things that we do want to leave behind. When we leave the pew, we want to leave sin behind but never the "Savior of Sinners." We want to leave frustration behind, but we also want to carry out faith. We want to leave depression behind, but we want to carry out divine deliverance.

The character depictions of familiar biblical icons and the application of current illustrations translate into an informative and enlightening teaching tool. As some readers are introduced for the first time to David and Goliath or many are reintroduced to Joseph, Hezekiah, and others, we are certain to gain insights into what we should or should not include as we carry the precious cargo of the gospel. As Christians, we are all on our way to our Father's house and we need to know what to carry and what to leave behind. We surely want to let those who are lost know that the first essential in packing is to be sure and include Jesus and his teachings in whatever plans we are making.

I highly recommend *From This Text* as a must-have resource for pastors, preachers, laity, and Christian educational instructors. The faith experiences of many well-known heroes of the Bible, as well as the parables of Jesus, are presented in an easy read-and-teach format that can be used as a starting point in developing your own inspiring lesson plans.

Sister Johnson couldn't have made it any simpler than what God has given her.

God bless you.
Pastor Alvin J. Noel, DTh
Author of *This Is IT (By Faith)*

Introduction

Have you ever sat on a church pew and listened to a great orator deliver a message with faultless elocution filled with profound spiritual doctrine that went right over your head? I grew up listening to Baptist preachers. Before reading the Scriptures related to their sermons, most Baptist preachers used the term "taking their text," which was followed by the announcement of the subject or title of the sermon.

The actual message was prefaced by one of the following phrases: "If you pray with me, I won't hold you long," "I'll be brief," and "This morning, I'm only going to take up a little of your time" or something to that effect. These declarations usually summoned an "amen" or two, as well as a few skeptical but good-natured chuckles from members of the congregation. No doubt, the chuckles came from members who were accustomed to these well-intended declarations rarely coming to fruition.

From the preaching perspective, the purpose of the sermon is to kindle a fire in the heart of the believer while advocating that they be not only hearers but also doers of the Word. When addressing the nonbeliever, the intent of the preacher's sermon is to fulfill the first step that leads to Salvation, and that is to allow the word to prick the heart of the nonbeliever. "How then shall they call on him in whom they have not believed? and how shall they believe in him of whom they have not heard? and how shall they hear without a preacher?" Romans 10:14 (KJV).

Bible study teachers may not be preachers. However, by using the Bible as the primary teaching tool, they are afforded the same opportunity of presenting the Gospel through lessons.

The "Sermon Starter" is a familiar resource used by ministers. *From This Text* is a concise resource that both preachers and Bible study teachers can use to develop lessons. The twenty-first-century illustrations in *From This Text* provide fresh starting points that allow instructors to incorporate their own inspired thoughts into the Bible lessons. An impactful lesson title plays a vital role in capturing students' interest. *From This Text* is filled with lesson titles that pique the reader's interest as well as scriptural references that provide various avenues of research for the instructor.

Lay speakers have become quite proficient understudies to preachers, and many can expound on topics with great enthusiasm. *From This Text* contains unique and interesting subject titles with a brief synopsis of each lesson. Bible Study Questions are presented after each summary. The summaries of these subjects offer insightful views of familiar Bible stories such as Solomon's wise decision over a custody battle, or the "all-you-can-eat seafood buffet in the wilderness," where 5,000 plus were fed—lessons whose messages are as vibrant today as they were upon their inception into biblical history.

I have been blessed by God to use the written word as a vehicle to minister to people. It has been ten years since I used that gift constructively and am humbled by the fact that God has allowed the Holy Spirit to once again bless me. I know that when you are blessed by God with a gift, you honor Him by how you use that gift. In spite of my slothfulness and disobedience, God showed mercy toward me and blessed me with another manuscript.

This material was written to illustrate how blessed we are to be able to attend worship services and Bible study classes and be taught God's word. Yet it also emphasizes our Christian accountability. God sends ministers to deliver the word to us and it is up to us not only to receive the Word but also to go back and read and reflect on the message. Every message that we hear has a hidden gem just for us, but we have to search for that meaning. I thank God for the gift of writing and the inspiration of the Holy Spirit. My hope and desire is that these reflections will play a small part in planting the seed of Salvation in someone's life.

Remember, when you listen to the minister's message or the lesson from the Bible teacher, don't leave what you have learned on the pew. God bless you!

Chapter 1: Don't Leave Character on the Pew

Topic: The Scent of Sacrificial Love

(A woman with an alabaster box anointed Jesus)

Scripture Reference: Matthew, Chapter 26

Insight: Never allow the opinions of others to dictate how much of your time and resources go to God.

"There came unto him a woman having an alabaster box of very precious ointment, and poured it on his head, as he sat at meat" Matthew 26:7 (KJV).

The Scripture does not give a definitive reference as to this woman's identity. However, scholars believe that Mary Magdalene, Mary of Bethany, and the woman rescued by Jesus as well as the woman with the alabaster box are all different women.

Her name is not as significant as her sacrifice. In this biblical account of events leading to the crucifixion of Jesus, it appears that this woman understood, more than the disciples did, the significance of giving reverence to Jesus. By anointing Jesus' body with this precious ointment from her alabaster box, she was demonstrating her unselfish love for her Lord. There was nothing too good for her to give to him.

"But when his disciples saw it, they had indignation, saying, To what purpose is this waste? For this ointment might have been sold for much, and given to the poor. When Jesus understood it, he said unto them, Why trouble ye the woman? For she hath wrought a good work upon me" Matthew 26:8-10 (KJV).

In spite of the ridicule and mumbling about her actions, the woman continued to anoint Jesus with oil. She could have easily allowed the words of the disciples to cause her to rethink what she was doing.

She could have allowed their words to make her feel guilty about this sacrificial act. She could have started to question her own motives. Yet her love for Christ overshadowed their pettiness. She truly understood and believed that Jesus would not be with them always. This seemed to be a point that the disciples could not grasp.

When the scent from the perfume filled the room it reached the nostrils of the guests in different ways. To Jesus, it was a sweet, welcoming smell. To the woman, it represented a sweet smell of release of her love for Christ. To the disciples and the Pharisees, it was a stench of waste and greed.

Were they really that concerned about the poor or, as some commentators suggest, only in lining their own pockets? Jesus chastised them and came to the woman's defense. He wanted them to realize that the perfume had not been wasted because she was preparing his body for burial.

Love is the antidote to injustice. The scent of this woman's sacrificial love offering would help Jesus to endure the false accusations brought against him. The scent of this woman's sacrifice would help him to withstand the inhumane treatment from the Roman soldiers. The scent of this sacrificial love offering would help him to bear the betrayal and denial he was about to experience.

Most of all, the scent of this woman's sacrificial love offering would help him to remember why he was carrying this cross up to Golgotha. The scent of this sacrificial love offering would remind him of the precious sweet smelling presence of his Father that awaited him in Heaven, after he (Jesus) gave his own sacrificial love offering for humanity.

Can you smell the scent of the wonderful sacrificial love offering that Jesus gave for you and me? He gave his best for us, and surely he deserved the perfume from this woman's alabaster box.

We can never repay the debt that we owe to Jesus. We cannot anoint his body as this woman did. However, we do have the opportunity to spread his message of love and allow others to enjoy the sweet scent of Salvation that we as Christians have received at the cross.

Bible Study Questions

1. Who was Jesus having dinner with when the woman with the alabaster box appeared? (Matthew 26:6, KJV)

2. What did the woman do with the precious ointment? (Matthew 26:7, KJV)
3. How did the disciples react to the actions of the woman? (Matthew 26:8-9, KJV)
4. How did Jesus defend the woman's actions? (Matthew 26:10, KJV)
5. What legacy in the Gospel did Jesus assign to the woman? (Matthew 26:13, KJV)

Topic: Casting Call: Lead Role—King of Israel
(Samuel anointed God's chosen one)
Scripture Reference: I Samuel, Chapter 16

Insight: Not listening to the voice of God leads to preconceived conclusions that often lead to danger.

"And the LORD said unto Samuel, How long wilt thou mourn for Saul, seeing I have rejected him from reigning over Israel? Fill thine horn with oil, and go, I will send thee to Jesse the Bethlehemite: For I have provided me a king among his sons" I Samuel 16:1 (KJV)

God instructed Samuel to fill his horn with oil and go to Jesse, the Bethlehemite and anoint one of his sons as king. Since Samuel was fearful that Saul would discover what he was doing, the Lord told Samuel to take a heifer for a sacrifice and call Jesse to the sacrifice.

God told Samuel that he would show him which of Jesse's sons to anoint.

When Samuel saw Eliab, he said, "Surely, this must be the one." No need for anymore auditions. The role of king has been filled. Samuel was looking at Eliab with his natural eye and he was only able to see his physical appearance. However, God was not interested in how he looked because God was able to see who he was. "But the LORD said to Samuel, 'Do not consider his appearance or his height, for I have rejected him. The LORD does not look at the things man looks at. Man looks at the outward appearance, but the LORD looks at the heart'" I Samuel 16:7 (NIV).

God had to remind Samuel that the auditions were already closed before he got to Jesse's home. In the latter part of verse 1 of I Samuel (KJV), God said, "For I have provided me a king among his sons." God already knew that David would be anointed king.

"Again, Jesse made seven of his sons to pass before Samuel. And Samuel said unto Jesse, The LORD hath not chosen these" I Samuel 16:10 (KJV). Of the seven sons who appeared before him, Samuel had to inform Jesse that not one of them was the chosen one. Samuel knew that God had not made a mistake, so there must be another son somewhere.

"And Samuel said unto Jesse, Are here all thy children? And he said, There remaineth yet the youngest, and, behold, he keepeth the sheep. And Samuel said unto Jesse, Send and fetch him: for we will not sit down till he come hither" I Samuel 16:11 (KJV).

When David came in from the field, God let Samuel know that David was the chosen one. "And he sent, and brought him in. Now he was ruddy, and withal of a beautiful countenance, and goodly to look to. And the LORD said, Arise, anoint him: for this is he. Then Samuel took the horn of oil, and anointed him in the midst of his brethren: and the Spirit of the LORD came upon David from that day forward. So Samuel rose up, and went to Ramah" I Samuel 16:12-13 (KJV).

We are not wise enough to judge people's hearts and therefore should not arrive at conclusions based solely on their physical appearance. Although David was the last son to audition, he won the starring role as king of Israel and received top billing. The marquee read: "A Man after God's Own Heart" —starring David as king of Israel.

Bible Study Questions

1. Did Samuel receive clear instructions regarding his mission to anoint a king? (I Samuel 16:1-3, KJV)
2. Why did Samuel think Eliab was God's choice for king? (I Samuel 16:6-7a, KJV)
3. How did God stop Samuel from making the wrong choice? (I Samuel 16:7b, KJV)

4. What verse described David's appearance? (I Samuel 16:12, KJV)
5. What happened to David at the moment Samuel anointed him with the oil? (I Samuel 16:13, KJV)

Topic: A Mother's Math
(Solomon's decision exposed the character of two women)
Scripture Reference: I Kings, Chapter 3, KJV

Insight: When true love is tested, character and courage are put on display.

"Then came there two women, that were harlots, unto the king, and stood before him. And the one woman said, O my lord, I and this woman dwell in one house; and I was delivered of a child with her in the house.

And it came to pass the third day after that I was delivered, that this woman was delivered also: and we were together; there was no stranger with us in the house, save we two in the house.

And this woman's child died in the night; because she overlaid it.

And she arose at midnight, and took my son from beside me, while thine handmaid slept, and laid it in her bosom, and laid her dead child in my bosom.

And when I rose in the morning to give my child suck, behold, it was dead: but when I had considered it in the morning, behold, it was not my son, which I did bear.

And the other woman said, Nay; but the living is my son, and the dead is thy son. And this said, No; but the dead is thy son, and the living is my son. Thus they spake before the king" I Kings 3:16-23 (KJV).

King Solomon prayed to God for an understanding heart to judge the people, and God blessed him with a wise and understanding heart like no other man possessed. "And the speech pleased the LORD, that Solomon had asked this thing" I Kings 3:10 (KJV).

King Solomon was presented with a custody battle. There were no witnesses to the incident, since the two women had been alone in the house with the babies. There were no DNA test kits available during that time. The women were harlots, so there were no character witnesses. Solomon had to rely on his wisdom. "And the king said, Divide the living child in two, and give half to the one, and half to the other" I Kings 3:25 (KJV).

The equation consisted of two women and one living child. Solomon knew that a real mother would do anything to protect her child. Solomon's proposal to divide the child separated the character of the two women. Before, they were both harlots; now one of them would become a mother. Before, they were both selfish; now one of them would be willing to sacrifice. "Then spake the woman whose the living child was unto the king, for her bowels yearned upon her son, and she said, O my lord, give her the living child, and in no wise slay it. But the other said, Let it be neither mine nor thine, but divide it" I Kings 3:26 (KJV).

Two portraits have been painted in this story. The first one is a portrait of death and deceit, and the second one is of love and sacrifice. When Solomon's solution was division, the true mother knew that she had to offer another way of solving the problem. She proposed subtraction. Since she was part of the equation, which consisted of herself, her child, and the harlot, she was willing to subtract herself from the equation, which would leave only two, but it would result in her child being alive.

At that point, necessitous faith entered into the situation. The true mother had to have faith that her decision was the right one and it was the best one to make for her child. The true mother's math solution was three minus one equals love. Because of her love for her child, she was willing to give him up to save his life.

She was blessed for her unselfishness when King Solomon ruled in her favor and reunited her with her son. Solomon knew by their responses that the identity of the true mother had been revealed. "Then the king answered and said, Give her the living child, and in no wise slay it: she is the mother thereof" I Kings 3:27.

Bible Study Questions

1. What attribute did Solomon request from God? (I Kings 3:9, KJV)
2. What accusation was made by the mother of the living child? (I Kings 3:19-21, KJV)
3. What proposal did Solomon offer to settle the dispute between the two harlots? (I Kings 3:25, KJV)
4. How did the true mother of the child react to Solomon's proposal? (I Kings 3:26, KJV)
5. What principle of math did the true mother use? (I Kings 3:26, KJV)

Topic: Look Both Ways before Crossing the Street
(A Good Samaritan stopped to help a stranger)
Scripture Reference: Luke, Chapter 10; John 13:35

Insight: All of our actions are rewarded according to God's word—nothing is hidden.

"And Jesus answering said, A certain man went down from Jerusalem to Jericho, and fell among thieves, which stripped him of his raiment, and wounded him, and departed, leaving him half dead. And by chance there came down a certain priest that way: and when he saw him, he passed by on the other side. And likewise a Levite, when he was at the place, came and looked on him, and passed by on the other side" Luke10:30-32 (KJV).

In our twenty-first-century culture, skepticism is one of the factors that affect our decisions as to whether we will or will not provide aid to others. There are so many con artists trying to extract favors and finances that we shy away from helping anyone. However, as Christians, we cannot just turn our heads and look the other way. When we give, we must give with the right intentions and leave the judgment up to God.

"But a certain Samaritan, as he journeyed, came where he was: and when he saw him, he had compassion on him, and went to him, and bound up his wounds, pouring in oil and wine, and set him on his own beast, and brought him to an inn, and took care of him. And on the morrow when he departed, he took out two pence, and gave them to the host, and said unto him, Take care of him; and whatsoever thou spendest more, when I come again, I will repay thee" Luke10:33-35 (KJV).

Both the priest and the Levite were aware of the teachings regarding caring for your neighbor, but they failed the test of charity. They had an opportunity to show kindness, but did not. Perhaps they had pressing appointments and felt it was not worth adding this stop to their busy agendas. Maybe, they were wearing their best suits and did not want to get dirty by stopping to help this man. Maybe they did not want to commit to long-term care of this poor man. Whatever the reason, they failed the test of charity.

We have to be very careful when judging people by the positions that they hold. Their true character is more likely to be exhibited when they are not under the scrutiny of the public eye. The priest and the Levite probably thought that no one would ever know that they passed by this man in the street without stopping to help. However, the all-seeing God was aware of their actions and He was looking at them at the same time they were looking away from this wounded man.

God has no respect of persons. We are all the same in his sight. God saw the stranger, the scammers and the Samaritan. We are all sinners saved by grace. We can only be recognized as true disciples when we follow the principle Jesus set for us. John13:35: "By this shall all men know that ye are my disciples, if ye have love one to another."

Bible Study Questions

1. What was the condition of the wounded man in the text? (Luke 10:30, KJV)
2. How did the priest and Levite incriminate themselves? (Luke 10:31-32, KVJ)
3. What was the Samaritan's first reaction to the wounded man? (Luke 10:33, KJV)
4. How did the Samaritan display charity? (Luke 10: 34, KJV)

5. Which action of the Samaritan could be considered above and beyond the call of duty? (Luke 10:35, KJV)

Chapter 2: Don't Leave Forgiveness on the Pew

Topic: Forgiveness Fueled by Faith

(Joseph forgave his brothers)

Scripture Reference: Genesis: Chapters 37, 41, 50

Insight: Forgiveness is one of the characteristics of Jesus that Christians should strive to emulate.

"And Joseph said unto them, Fear not: for am I in the place of God? But as for you, ye thought evil against me; but God meant it unto good, to bring to pass, as it is this day, to save much people alive" Genesis 50:19-20.

When we realize that the actions of others that cause us pain and grief are a reflection of their lack of compassion and understanding of Christian principles, we will find it easier to forgive them.

If there was ever a person who had a reason to hold a grudge, that was Joseph. His father's decision to give him a splendid garment of many colors only added fuel to the fire of jealousy that his brothers had for Joseph. Joseph may have unknowingly added the last piece of kindling by sharing his dreams of dominance. This increased Joseph's brothers' jealousy and they sought to destroy him. "Come now therefore, and let us slay him, and cast him into some pit, and we will say, Some evil beast hath devoured him: and we shall see what will become of his dreams" Genesis 37:20 (KJV)

Joseph's brothers allowed their jealousy to drive them to plot the death of Joseph. Reuben convinced them not to kill him, but instead to cast him into the pit in the wilderness with no water. When a company of Ishmaelites came from Gilead on their way to Egypt, Judah saw a way to make a profit by selling Joseph to them for twenty pieces of silver.

Their profit paled in comparison to the prestige, power, and prosperity that were in store for Joseph. Joseph began a "P" journey. He went from the pit to Potiphar's house, from Potiphar's house to prison, and from prison to the pharaoh's palace. His God-given ability to interpret dreams paved the way for him to become the ruler over all the land of Egypt. "And Pharaoh said unto Joseph, I am Pharaoh, and without thee shall no man lift up his hand or foot in all the land of Egypt" Genesis 41:44 (KJV).

When famine spread over the land, Joseph's father, Jacob, sent Joseph's ten brothers to Egypt to buy corn. Joseph recognized his brothers, but he did not let them know who he was. After putting his brothers through a series of tests, he eventually revealed himself to them. After moving his entire family to Egypt, including his younger brother, Benjamin, and his father, Joseph's father, Jacob, died. Joseph's brothers feared that he would seek revenge and sell them into slavery or order that they be killed. Joseph could have easily had his brothers killed after Jacob died, but Joseph realized that God was the true judge.

Joseph had encountered quite a few situations that tested his faith. He had been sold into slavery by his brothers. He had been lied on by Potiphar's wife. His kindness to the pharaoh's butler was forgotten for two years. Amid all these undeserved circumstances, Joseph kept his faith. Joseph had surrendered his will to God's will, and it was not in God's will for him to seek revenge against his brothers, but to show forgiveness. If Jesus could forgive the wrong that was done to him from the cross, we can surely forgive the hurt feelings we suffer at the hands of others.

Bible Study Questions

1. What emotions led Joseph's brothers to plot his death? (Genesis 37:4, 5 and 11, KJV)
2. What was the first stop in Joseph's journey to the palace? (Genesis 37:20, KJV)
3. What special gift did God give Joseph? (Genesis 40:8, KJV)
4. What emotion caused Joseph to forgive his brothers? (Genesis 50:20-21, KJV)
5. What did Joseph's father say to him when he saw that he was alive? (Genesis 46:30, KJV)

Topic: Where Are Your Accusers?

(Jesus intervened as a woman faced stoning)

Scripture Reference: John, Chapter 8; Isaiah 1:18 (KJV)

Insight: We harshly judge others but show no reluctance when justifying our own sins.

When the scribes and Pharisees brought a woman who had been caught in the very act of adultery to Jesus, they were not only concerned with having the woman punished, but they were testing Jesus to see if he would abide by the Law of Moses. The law required that a woman caught in adultery be stoned. "This they said, tempting him, that they might have to accuse him. But Jesus stooped down, and with his finger wrote on the ground, as though he heard them not" John 8:6 (KJV).

When Jesus appeared to be ignoring the scribes and Pharisees, they continued to question him. There is no mention as to what the woman was doing at this point. She was no doubt attempting to shield her body from the anticipated barrage of stones that would be coming her way. Of course, she knew the law, but she, like many others, had given in to the desires of the flesh. However, unlike some others who had not been caught, she had been discovered. Sound familiar?

This woman probably thought that Jesus would tell the crowd to uphold the Law of Moses and that she would be stoned. However, at that, point Jesus did not address the woman's guilt, but instead turned his attention to the crowd. The statement that Jesus made diverted the attention from the accusation of the woman to the indictment of the crowd's character. "So when they continued asking him, he lifted up himself, and said unto them, He that is without sin among you, let him first cast a stone at her" John 8:7 (KJV).

At that moment, it was as though someone had pulled the fire alarm. The accusers scattered, and only Jesus and the woman remained. "When Jesus had lifted up himself, and saw none but the woman, he said unto her, Woman, where are those thine accusers? Hath no man condemned thee?" John 8:10 (KJV). Where were her accusers? Eaten up by their own guilty consciences, and knowing that they had sinned and perhaps were guilty of the same sin as this woman, they were compelled to walk away.

The woman was probably waiting for Jesus to assume the role of accuser. However, to her surprise, after she answered the question from Jesus about her accusers, Jesus responded with forgiveness and not condemnation. "She said, No man, Lord. And Jesus said unto her, Neither do I condemn thee: go, and sin no more" John 8:11 (KJV). If anyone was in a position to condemn her, it was Jesus. Jesus was sinless and was the only righteous judge.

We categorize sins based on our opinions. We think lying is a small sin and adultery is a big sin. Gossiping and backbiting are not really sins; they fall in the category of shortcomings. If God says all have sinned and come short of the glory of God, then all have sinned and all sins are sins.

There is a stage play that was developed into a movie, titled, *Diary of a Mad Black Woman*, written by the well-known playwright Tyler Perry. After a bitter divorce, the main female character in the film enters into a new relationship but is too guarded to allow a new man into her life. When the new love of her life proposes marriage, one of the lines from his proposal is "I can love you past your pain." It was a very eloquent line; however, as human beings, those words of commitment would better serve the movie script than real life.

We are not capable of unconditional love. Only Jesus can give unconditional love. Jesus loves us with "no-matter-what love." Jesus loves us no matter what we have done; no matter what we are doing; no matter what the situation; no matter what anyone else says or thinks about us; no matter what we have or don't have; no matter what we look like, whether we're fat or thin; no matter what our background is; no matter the condition of our finances. No matter what, Jesus still loves us. I thank Jesus for his "no-matter-what love."

Jesus can truly love us in spite of our past and present. Even though we try everything before we try Jesus, he is still waiting, standing ready to wipe away the tears, heal the hurt, and give us peace. In Isaiah 1:18, we find the words, "Come now, and let us reason together, saith the LORD: though your sins be as scarlet, they shall be as white as snow; though they be red like crimson, they shall be as wool."

Bible Study Questions

1. Why did the scribes and Pharisees bring this woman to Jesus? (John 8:3-4, KJV)
2. What was the Law of Moses concerning women caught in adultery? (John 8:5, KJV)
3. How did Jesus respond to their request that the woman be stoned? (John 8:7, KJV)
4. What did the crowd do after they were convicted by their own consciences? (John 8:9, KJV)
5. What did Jesus instruct the woman to do since there were no longer any accusers present? (John 8:11, KJV)

Topic: I'll Always Be Your Father
(The prodigal son returned home)
Scripture Reference: Luke 15:11-32; John 3:16

Insight: The greatest seed to plant in a child is a seed of promise.

Many young people feel invincible and cannot wait to be out on their own. Many decisions that our children make are not in their best interests. However, as parents, we can only pray that God will be with them, and when they really need us, we have to be there with outstretched arms and forgiving hearts.

The story of the prodigal son is one of the most well-known parables in the Bible. Of course, there are no details provided as to what took place prior to the son's request for his inheritance. No matter what conflicts were going on, there seemed to be little objection from the father to his younger son's request. Of course, the father probably gave his son tons of advice about being careful, frugal, and, of course, not to forget to keep God in his life.

After the younger son received his portion, the Scripture states that shortly thereafter, he wasted it all. He evidently forgot any advice his father had given him. "And not many days after the younger son gathered all together, and took his journey into a far country, and there wasted his substance with riotous living" Luke 15:13 (KJV). We are not given specifics concerning his riotous living. However, we can safely assume that he was surrounded by people who were willing to help convince him that he was having a good time as long as he had money to spend.

Just how low did he go after he became penniless? "And he went and joined himself to a citizen of that country; and he sent him into his fields to feed swine" Luke 15:15 (KJV). He was actually eating the husks that the swine ate. His so-called friends seemed to have disappeared because he received no support from anyone. Of course, he had not planned on his life coming to this. That is the key phrase, "had not planned." His only plans were to have a good time and to live in the moment.

The Scripture says that when he came to himself, he began to think about how his father's servants had food to spare. At this point, he actually came up with a plan. His plan was to return to his father and admit that he had made a mistake and ask to be allowed to work as one of the hired servants. "I will arise and go to my father, and will say unto him, Father, I have sinned against heaven, and before thee. And am no more worthy to be called thy son: make me as one of thy hired servants" Luke 15:18-19 (KJV).

Advocates of the "tough love" philosophy would probably have recommended that the father allow the son to work as a hired servant so that he could reflect on the improper choices he had made in the past. However, the son's return was not met with condemnation from his father or "I told you so" statements.

The father was not concerned about teaching his son a lesson; he was interested in celebrating his son's return. "But the father said to his servants, Bring forth the best robe, and put it on him; and put a ring on his hand, and shoes on his feet: And bring hither the fatted calf, and kill it; and let us be merry: For this my son was dead, and is alive again; he was lost, and is found. And they began to be merry" Luke 15:22-24 (KJV).

Just as this father in the parable welcomed his son with outstretched arms, God is standing with outstretched arms, waiting for us to come to him. God is willing to forgive us of our sins. As parents, we must be willing to forgive our children as well as forgive others even when we feel that their actions are unforgivable. Remember the sacrifice that Jesus made on the cross so that we could be forgiven.

God is not concerned about our past because he has established our position through his own Son's death on the cross. "For God so loved the world, that he gave his only begotten Son, that whosoever believeth in him should not perish, but have everlasting life" John 3:16 (KJV).

Bible Study Questions

1. What did the prodigal son do with the money he had received from his father? (Luke 15:13, KJV)
2. What occupation did he pursue once he became penniless? (Luke 15:15, KJV)
3. What do you think the words "when he came to himself" meant in Luke 15:17? (Personal Reflection)
4. What was the father's reaction to his son's return? (Luke 15:22-24, KJV)
5. Do you really believe that God is as forgiving as the father in this story? (Romans 5:8, KJV)

Topic: The Whole Truth, Nothing but the Truth
(A woman at the well met Jesus)
Scripture Reference: John 4:5-29; Isaiah 26:3

Insight: Even eight glasses of water a day will not quench your thirst like the Living Water.

"There cometh a woman of Samaria to draw water: Jesus saith unto her, Give me to drink" John 4:7 (KJV).

As Jesus was sitting on Jacob's well, a woman of Samaria came to draw water. As the conversation between Jesus and the Samaritan woman continued, she expressed concern over him, asking her for water because he was a Jew and she was a Samaritan. Jesus explained to her that if she only knew who she was speaking to, she would not be bringing up their differences, but instead would be trying to get the water that he had to offer. "Jesus answered and said unto her, If thou knewest the gift of God, and who it is that saith to thee, Give me to drink; thou wouldest have asked of him, and he would have given thee living water" John 4:10 (KJV).

Jesus began to redirect the conversation from the water that would satisfy physical thirst to the water that satisfies the soul. "But whosoever drinketh of the water that I shall give him shall never thirst; but the water that I shall give him shall be in him a well of water springing up into everlasting life" John 4:14.

As Jesus spoke of this water, the woman desired to have this water. "The woman saith unto him, Sir, give me this water, that I thirst not, neither come hither to draw" John 4:15 (KJV). At this point, the woman did not realize that Jesus was not speaking about water that would quench physical thirst. Once she asked for the water, it was important that she realized that in order to receive the water that Jesus was offering, she would need to repent. So Jesus instructed her to go and get her husband and come back.

She then told Jesus that she had no husband. At that point, she did not volunteer any details about her marital situation. Perhaps she thought that Jesus would think she was a widow, or better yet, that she had never been married. She did not realize that lies could not persist in the presence of Jesus. She answered, "I have no husband."

If this had been an encounter with any other stranger, she could have readily offered excuses that her husband was not at home, or even defiantly said that she had a common law husband or that she had a "sugar daddy," a man who she considered her husband because he took good care of her. But because she had encountered Jesus, the excuses did not come so easily.

"The woman answered and said, I have no husband" John 4:17 (KJV). Jesus let her know that he knew the truth about her life. Jesus said unto her, "Thou hast well said, I have no husband: For thou hast had five husbands; and he whom thou now hast is not thy husband: in that saidst thou truly" John 4:18 (KJV).

At this point, the woman thought that Jesus was a prophet. Her understanding was that the Messiahs would come in the future and let them know how and where to worship God. Jesus told her that he was Christ. "Jesus saith unto her, I that speak unto thee am he" John 4:26

(KJV). Once you have a real encounter with Christ, it will not only result in conviction that leads to the repentance of your sins, but you will not be able to conceal your joy. "The woman then left her water pot, and went her way into the city, and saith to the men, Come, see a man, which told me all things that ever I did: is not this the Christ?" John 4:28-29 (KJV).

Have you ever experienced a thirst in your soul? When you experience this type of thirst, it is unlike any other that you will experience. I went through a spiritual drought, and just when I felt like water was in sight, it would be snatched away. I tried blaming Satan, but soon realized that I was allowing his devices to work because I was not exercising the power that God had given me to defeat him. Like many Christians, I was lured into the false security of Christian longevity and the belief that I had developed immunity from satanic forces.

I discovered that it did not matter that I had joined the church fifty-six years ago, and or how long a shadow my attendance cast on the door of the church. It did not matter how many committees I sat on or how many times my name appeared on programs; I was still susceptible to Satan's devices. The reason I could not satisfy the thirst of my soul was because I had started to sip on the word instead of consuming it regularly and in large quantities.

Some days, I would not drink at all, and then on other days, I would take a quick sip and keep skipping on my way. Thank God that the Holy Spirit took over and interceded when I prayed and acknowledged that I didn't even know what to pray for. God then allowed me to be drenched in the Water of the Word. Only a sincere staying relationship with Jesus will ensure that Satan's devices do not ultimately succeed. "Thou wilt keep him in perfect peace, whose mind is stayed on thee: because he trusteth in thee" Isaiah 26:3 (KJV).

Bible Study Questions

1. Why did the woman think it was strange for Jesus to ask her for water? (John 4:9, KJV)
2. What did Jesus tell the woman about living water? (John 4:13-14, KJV)
3. How did the woman respond when Jesus told her to go and get her husband? (John 4:17, KJV)
4. Who did the woman think Jesus was when he began to tell her about her life? (John 4:19, KJV)
5. After the woman's encounter with Jesus, why did she leave her water pot to go into the city? (John 4:28-29, KJV)

Chapter 3: Don't Leave Trust on the Pew

Topic: A Fiery Furnace Fashion Show

(The three Hebrew boys trusted their fate to God)

Scripture Reference: Daniel, Chapter 3 (KJV); Ephesians 6:13-17

Insight: In this twenty-first century, standing up for the truth is not popular in society.

A golden image of King Nebuchadnezzar was erected and everyone was instructed to bow down to the image. The punishment for not obeying was a free trip to the fiery furnace. However, three courageous Hebrew boys refused to bow to the king's image.

"Shadrach, Meshach, and Abednego, answered and said to the king, O Nebuchadnezzar, we are not careful to answer thee in this matter. If it be so, our God whom we serve is able to deliver us from the burning fiery furnace, and he will deliver us out of thine hand, O king. But if not, be it known unto thee, O king, that we will not serve thy gods, nor worship the golden image which thou hast set up" Daniel 3:16-18 (KJV).

One of the greatest fashion shows in history was not held on the runways of Paris or New York. And as astounding as it was, there was not one female model in the fashion show. The fashion show was held on the Runway of Righteousness in the fiery furnace. No longer using the stage names given to them, the Hebrew boys walked the runway as Hananiah, Mishael, and Azariah.

They were modeling fashions that would never go out of style. They had on the breastplate of righteousness. Their feet were shod with the preparation of the gospel of peace. They carried the shield of faith so that they were able to quench the fiery darts of the wicked. They wore the helmet of salvation and carried the sword of the Spirit, which is the Word of God. They were the best-dressed boys in the furnace. They had on the whole armor of God (See Ephesians 6:13-17, KJV).

Just when Nebuchadnezzar thought that the fashion show was over, he looked and saw that instead of three people on the runway there were actually four. "Then Nebuchadnezzar the king was astonished, and rose up in haste, and spake, and said unto his counselors, Did not we cast three men bound into the midst of the fire? They answered and said unto the king, True, O king. He answered and said, Lo, I see four men loose, walking in the midst of the fire, and they have no hurt; and the form of the fourth is like the Son of God" Daniel 3: 24-25 (KJV).

There was only one designer who could walk on the Runway of Righteousness, and that was the King of Kings. God, the creator and designer of the very universe, had stepped into the fiery furnace to take his rightful place as the God who answered the prayers of Hananiah, Mishael, and Azariah.

Are you wearing the whole armor of God? This attire is not a fad. It will never go out of style. It is fireproof, moth-proof, and waterproof. These garments are better than anything ever designed by Giorgio Armani or Versace. They are tailor made to fit every believer. The inside label reads:

- Handmade by God
- No defects
- No cleaning necessary—already blood-washed
- Manufacturer's warranty—God will replace at the End of Time

Bible Study Questions

1. What orders had Nebuchadnezzar given regarding the golden image? (Daniel 3:4-6, KJV)
2. What were the Hebrew boy's names before they were changed by the prince of the eunuchs? (Daniel 1:6-7, KJV)
3. When asked who would deliver them from the furnace, how did the Hebrew boys respond? (Daniel 3:16-17, KJV)
4. How was the resolve of the Hebrew boys displayed? (Daniel 3:18, KJV)

5. When he looked into the furnace, how many men did Nebuchadnezzar see? (Daniel 3:24-25, KJV)

Topic: An Anointed Alarm System
(David trusted God to supply peace)
Scripture Reference: Psalm 4:8; Philippians 4:6-7; John 5:14-15; Psalm 4:3; Psalm 121:2-4

Insight: The only inexhaustible source of safety, security, and peace of mind is God.

"I will both lay me down in peace, and sleep: for thou, LORD, only makest me dwell in safety" Psalm 4:8 (KJV).

Today, we talk about being under pressure and being stressed out. But the challenges that we face today cannot compare to the situations that David faced. He was engaged in war with one enemy army after another. He had to flee from his own son, Absalom, who was trying to kill him. It was a pretty sure bet that when David's head hit the pillow, the only way that he got a good night's sleep was with God's intervention.

Many of us have elaborate security systems that we rely on for protection. We have signed up for security services with ADT Home Security or other well-known home security companies. We have installed burglar bars and panic alarms. Even these precautions will not stop a determined burglar. These measures are no guarantee that we will have peace of mind.

There is no security system in the world that surpasses the protection that God provides for us while we are asleep during the night. In Philippians 4: 6-7, we are told how to secure that peace. “Be careful for nothing; but in everything by prayer and supplication with thanksgiving let your requests be made known unto God. And the peace of God, which passeth all understanding, shall keep your hearts and minds through Christ Jesus.”

There is no contract that we have to sign in order to request security from God. We are told in I John 5:14-15 that we only need to ask. “And this is the confidence that we have in him, that, if we ask anything according to his will, he heareth us: And if we know that he hear us, whatsoever we ask, we know that we have the petitions that we desired of him.” David truly believed that he belonged to God and that the Lord would hear him when he called on Him. “But know that the Lord hath set apart him that is godly for himself: the Lord will hear when I call unto him” Psalm 4:3 (KJV).

During the Western days on cattle drives, the cowboys took turns in staying up at night to watch the herd. They would divide up the watches and one person would keep watch while the others slept. They were concerned about cattle rustlers stealing the cattle and wild animals harming the herd.

From David's 121st Psalm, it is evident that he discovered that there was no need for him to stay awake because he knew God as a keeper. "My help cometh from the Lord, which made heaven and earth. He will not suffer thy foot to be moved: he that keepeth thee will not slumber. Behold he that keepeth Israel shall neither slumber nor sleep" Psalm121: 2-4.

Before we lie down at night, we have to go to God in prayer. This is how we engage our security system. We have to pray on this side of midnight because we do not know if we will wake up to see another day. The Bible tells us that no man knows the day or hour when Jesus will return.

When we have a personal relationship with Jesus Christ, we know that God is faithful to his word. He has promised never to leave us or forsake us. When we stay in communication with God, when sleepless nights come, we will know where to turn. God is always listening for our prayers.

Bible Study Questions

1. Why was David able to sleep peacefully? (Psalm 4:8, KJV)
2. Are we able to reach God at any time day or night? (Psalm 121:4, KJV)
3. How do we reach God? (Hebrews 4:16 KJV)

4. What is the meaning of the phrase "that passeth all understanding"? (Philippians 4:6 KJV)
5. Is there anything keeping you awake at night? (Personal Reflection)

Topic: Will You Choose Curtain Number One, Two, or Three?
(David reacted to God's message, delivered by the prophet Gad)
Scripture Reference: II Samuel, Chapter 24:10-16

Insight: Only God can judge the present without considering the past.

"David said to Gad, 'I am in deep distress. Let us fall into the hands of the LORD, for his mercy is great; but do not let me fall into the hands of men'" II Samuel 24:14 (NIV).

Before the show *Deal or No Deal* burst onto the game show scene, the television game show *Let's Make a Deal* debuted in 1963. The last segment of the show featured contestants faced with the decision to keep the money or prize that they had in their possession and walk away or trade it in for a chance to see what was behind curtain number one, two, or three. They had no idea what was behind the curtains, but most of them were willing to risk the prize that they initially won to find out if they could get something of greater value.

In some scenarios, their decisions proved profitable and the items behind the chosen curtains were of greater value than what they had risked. However, in some cases, the items behind the curtains were worthless and the contestants regretted having made the decision.

David had sinned by numbering the people and had forgotten that the people God had given him to rule over as king were not his, but everyone and everything belonged to God. David was beginning to have more faith in his own power and less faith in God's power.

Unlike the contestants participating in the game shows, God was not making a deal with David. David would have to be punished for his sin. David could not simply say, "I am sorry," and walk away. He had to choose what was behind curtain number one, two, or three.

God did, however, give David an advantage. God sent the prophet Gad to tell David what was behind each curtain. "So Gad came to David, and told him, and said unto him, Shall seven years of famine come unto thee in thy land? or wilt thou flee three months before thine enemies, while they pursue thee? or that there be three days' pestilence in thy land? now advise, and see what answer I shall return to him that sent me" II Samuel 24:13 (KJV).

David knew that God was a merciful God, and that whatever the punishment was, he would be better off in God's hands. He did not want to leave his fate up to man, so David chose curtain number three. "So the Lord sent a pestilence upon Israel from the morning even to the time appointed: and there died of the people from Dan even to Beersheba seventy thousand men. As the angel was about to destroy

Jerusalem, the Lord said, “it is enough: stay now thine hand” II Samuel 24:15-16a.

God is so merciful that he will only allow us to go through suffering for a certain period of time. How many times has God intervened right on time, when it seemed as though our lives were falling apart? Just as God had to punish David, we, too, have to be chastised when we do wrong.

Thank God that as Christians, we are not at the mercies of the principalities and powers of this world. Think carefully before you choose what is behind man’s curtains; you are always better off in God’s hands. Remember that a Christian’s fall is padded by God’s mercy.

Bible Study Questions

1. Should we expect God to chastise us when we do wrong? (Hebrews 12:6-8, KJV)
2. What three punishment choices did God give David? (II Samuel 24:13, KJV)
3. Which of the three choices did David accept, and why? (II Samuel 24:14-15, KJV)
4. Is it wise to put our faith in man’s judgment? (Numbers 23:19, KJV)

5. Have you ever reached the brink of suffering and witnessed God's intervention? (Personal Reflection)

Topic: Ammunition of Choice—Jehovah Stones
(David used a stone to defeat Goliath)
Scripture Reference: I Samuel, Chapter 17

Insight: Uncompromising faith is a characteristic of Christian maturity.

The problems that we face in today's society seem insurmountable and leave us feeling overwhelmed; however, even today, the story of David and Goliath offers us glimmers of hope.

The Scripture tells us that David took five smooth stones out of the brook and put them into his bag. "And he took his staff in his hand, and chose him five smooth stones out of the brook, and put them in a shepherd's bag which he had, even in a scrip; and his sling was in his hand: and he drew near to the Philistine" I Samuel 17:40 (KJV).

David's faith could be called uncompromising faith. David was able to retrieve positive reinforcement from his own faith archives. David allowed his past experiences with the faithfulness of God to empower him. David believed that there were no impossibilities with God. He did not fear Goliath because of his faith in God.

Before Saul allowed David to go and fight, he first put his armor on David and gave him his sword. "David fastened on his sword over the tunic and tried walking around, because he was not accustomed to them. 'I cannot go in these,' he said to Saul, 'because I am not used to them.' So he took them off" I Samuel 17:39 (NIV). In the King James Version, it says, "…for I have not proved them."

David's weapon of choice was a slingshot. This was something that he was accustomed to using. This had proven to be an adequate weapon for him in the past. Many times, we want to try new things simply because somebody else said that it worked for them. However, if you have a proven method for approaching and resolving a situation that God has already shown you and it yielded positive results, then don't be foolish and abandon that method.

Goliath was upset and insulted that a boy had been sent out to fight him. However, Goliath underestimated God's representative. When David told Goliath that he came in the name of the Lord, he was referring to the Lord Jehovah.

Every stone that David had in his shepherd's bag represented one of the names of the Lord. The first stone was the stone of Jehovah-Shammah, the Lord Is Present. David knew that if God had been with him as he watched his father's sheep, God would be with him now. The second stone was the stone of Jehovah-Shalom, the Lord Our Peace. God would bring peace from this warring for His people.

The third stone was the stone of Jehovah-Tsidkenu, the Lord of Our Righteousness.

David knew that he was in the will of God, and although he was young, he had sought God's righteousness. The fourth stone was the stone of Jehovah-Jireh, the Lord Our Provider. David knew that God had never failed him before and had always provided everything that he needed.

The fifth stone was the stone of Jehovah-Nissi, the Lord Our Banner. The Lord promised to carry a banner before us into battle and David knew that God's banner had gone before him when he battled the lion and the bear, and it would go before him as he battled Goliath.

Although David had five stones, it only took one stone to defeat Goliath. It did not matter which stone David chose from his bag to place in his sling. He was coming against Goliath in the name of the Lord Jehovah. "And David put his hand in his bag, and took thence a stone, and slang it, and smote the Philistine in his forehead, that the stone sunk into his forehead; and he fell upon his face to the earth" I Samuel 17:49 (KJV).

Can't is a crippling contraction, which displays hopelessness. Can't uses the crutches of negativity to manipulate our actions. Faith is the component that can knock the crutches from under "can't." When you face gigantic problems in your life, remember how one stone brought down a giant.

Bible Study Questions

1. What are the five names of God discussed in this Faith Experience? (Ezekiel 48:35, Judges 6:24, Jeremiah 23:6, Genesis 22:14, Exodus 17:15, KJV)
2. Can you testify to knowing God by any of these five names? (Personal Reflection)
3. Why did David prefer a sling to a sword? (I Samuel 17:38-3, KJV)
4. Why was Goliath upset that David had been sent to challenge him? (I Samuel 17:42-43, KJV)
5. What gave David the confidence to believe that he could defeat Goliath? (I Samuel 17:34-37, KJV)

Chapter 4: Don't Leave Courage on the Pew

Topic: Starting a Fire with Water-Soaked Wood

(God sent a fire for Elijah's sacrifice)

Scripture Reference: I Kings, Chapter 18, verses from NIV and KJV

Insight: Christians are not immune to life's challenges and difficulties.

The NIV version of the Bible describes the face-off between Elijah and the prophets of Baal as follows:

22 Then Elijah said to them, "I am the only one of the
LORD's prophets left, but Baal has four hundred and fifty prophets.
23Get two bulls for us. Let Baal's prophets choose one for themselves,
and let them cut it into pieces and put it on the wood but not set fire to
it. I will prepare the other bull and put it on the wood but not set fire to
it. 24Then you call on the name of your god, and I will call on the name
of the LORD. The god who answers by fire—he is God."

Having been created as free-will beings, God allows us to make our own choice as to whether or not we will serve Him."Elijah went before the people and said, 'How long will you waiver between two opinions? If the LORD is God, follow him; but if Baal is God, follow him.' But the people said nothing" I Kings 18:21 (NIV).

The test of fire was proposed between Elijah and the 450 prophets of Baal. When the prophets of Baal failed the test and displayed their frustration by destroying the altar that held their sacrifice, Elijah repaired the altar and started his preparation.

"And he put the wood in order, and cut the bullock in pieces, and laid him on the wood, and said, Fill four barrels with water, and pour it on the burnt sacrifice, and on the wood.

And he said, Do it the second time. And they did it the second time. And he said, Do it the third time. And they did it the third time.

And the water ran roundabout the altar; and he filled the trench also with water" I Kings 18:33-35 (KJV).

When preparing his sacrifice, Elijah wanted to ensure that there could be no doubt of God's power. He had water from four barrels poured over the meat, not once but three times, until the water ran roundabout the altar. Imagine how difficult it would be for a human being to start a fire with wood that had been soaked with water. Elijah's faith in God's power was so great that he factored in a greater degree of difficulty. Elijah knew that God majored in the impossible.

"And it came to pass at the time of the offering of the evening sacrifice, that Elijah the prophet came near, and said, LORD God of Abraham, Isaac, and of Israel, let it be known this day that thou art

God in Israel, and that I am thy servant, and that I have done all these things at thy word.

Hear me, O LORD, hear me, that this people may know that thou art the LORD God, and that thou hast turned their heart back again.

Then the fire of the LORD fell, and consumed the burnt sacrifice, and the wood, and the stones, and the dust, and licked up the water that was in the trench.

And when all the people saw it, they fell on their faces: and they said, The LORD, he is the God; the LORD, he is the God" I Kings 18:36-39 (KJV).

Many times, the situations in our lives seem difficult. Just when we think that things can't get any worse, something happens to compound the problem. If we look closely at the situation, we may discover that God has allowed water to be poured on our wood. God does this so that there can be no doubt that He and He alone provided the solutions to our problem. Anyone can take dry kindling and start a fire, but achieving the same results with wood that has been soaked continuously in water would be viewed as a miracle. When we face what appears to be a stack of water-soaked impossibilities, trust God and watch as he uses a match of mercy and starts a blaze filled with the solutions to our problems.

Bible Study Questions

1. What test was used by Elijah and the prophets of Baal to establish the true God? (I Kings 18:22-24, KJV)
2. What happened when the prophets of Baal prayed to their gods for fire? (I Kings 18:25-29, KJV)
3. What was the significance of the stones that Isaiah chose to build the altar on for the sacrifice? (I Kings 18:31, KJV).
4. Before praying to God to send fire, what did Isaiah do to the wood? (I Kings 18:33-35, KJV)
5. What happened when the fire came down from Heaven? (I Kings 18:38, KJV)

Topic: Conquering Fear with a Heart of Faith
(The two optimists—Joshua and Caleb)
Scripture Reference: Numbers 13:17-33; 14:1-38; II Timothy 1:7

Insight: Outside influences based on negativity are counterproductive to a Christian's growth.

"And there we saw the giants, the sons of Anak, which come of the giants: and we were in our own sight as grasshoppers, and so we were in their sight" Numbers13:33 (KJV).

There are many negative branches that grow from a tree of fear. One of the branches is intimidation. Faith in God's Word will allow us to remove the branch of intimidation and enable us to uproot the tree of fear.

The purpose of a spy is to gather information without being detected. The twelve spies that Moses sent from the twelve tribes of Israel were assigned to go and search the land of Canaan and determine if the land could be taken. All but two of the spies brought back negative reports. Not only were the reports of the ten spies negative, but the reports were based on supposition and fear.

Because of their inadequate faith, in Numbers 13:33, the ten spies referred to themselves as grasshoppers. They came to the conclusion that the sons of Anak saw them the same way; yet there is no documentation that the sons of Anak actually saw them. Numbers 13:32 referred to the vastness of the land, "it is a land that eateth up the inhabitants thereof." Surely, if the spies had been seen by the sons of Anak, the spies would have been killed. Therefore, we can conclude that the statement, "and so we were the same in their sight" is based on supposition.

As Christians, we should only be concerned about how God sees us. We waste our time worrying about how courageous we appear in the eyes of men. We may look like grasshoppers in the sight of men, but to God, we are more than conquerors. "For God hath not given us the spirit of fear; but of power, and of love, and of a sound mind" II Timothy1:7 (KJV). The ten spies lacked faith in God's ability to give them the land. They magnified the problem instead of magnifying the power of God. No wonder they felt so small and inadequate.

First of all, they were sent by God and they had no reason to fear for their safety or doubt their success. If the spies looked like grasshoppers to the giants, then the giants surely appeared as gnats to God. The ten spies were not able to grasp the awesome power of God and were therefore only allowed a glimpse of the Promised Land.

The ten spies could not see beyond their present circumstances. The fear and the lack of faith of the ten spies began to infect the congregation. "And all the children of Israel murmured against Moses and against Aaron: and the whole congregation said unto them, Would God that we had died in the land of Egypt! Or would God we had died in this wilderness!" Numbers 14:2 (KJV).

Although not specifically reported, there was widespread short-term memory loss among this group of former Passover participants, Red Sea refugees, and Manna from Heaven diners. If they had just remembered the mighty acts of God, these giants would have appeared to them as ants.

The presence of fear perpetuates pessimistic faith. That statement may sound like a paradox; however, there is such a thing as pessimistic faith. A pessimist has faith in failure. A pessimist truly believes that negativity is the dominant force in every situation. Therefore, fear feeds pessimistic faith. This is the type of faith that the ten spies demonstrated when surveying and reporting on what they saw in the Land of Canaan.

Caleb and Joshua tried to convince the people that it was a land that could be possessed because God wanted them to have the land. "And they spake unto all the company of the children of Israel, saying, The land, which we passed through to search it, is an exceeding good land. If the LORD delight in us, then he will bring us into this land, and give it us; a land which floweth with milk and honey" Numbers 14:7-8 (KJV).

Caleb and Joshua were the only two of the twelve who returned from the land of Canaan and believed that the land could be conquered. Many times, we overdramatize situations because of our lack of faith.

Joshua, Caleb, and the other ten spies looked at the same things in the land. However, Joshua and Caleb washed the sleep of fear out of the corners of their eyes. Joshua and Caleb took off the dark sunglasses of despair. They put in their specially made "contact lenses of faith in the Lord." Joshua and Caleb were able to clearly see that God was the great God, Jehovah-Nissi, and would carry a banner before them into battle.

God did not allow the people from twenty years and older who did not believe that the land could be possessed and who murmured against Him to live to see the Promised Land. The unbelievers had to wander in the wilderness one year for every day that the land of

Canaan had been searched and reported unfavorably by the ten spies. Forty years later, Joshua and Caleb entered the Promised Land with the children of the unbelievers. They were certainly not grasshoppers when they entered the beautiful land of Canaan, but instead stood as Giants of Faith.

Bible Study Questions

1. What process did Moses use when choosing the twelve spies to send to the land of Canaan? (Numbers 13:1-3, KJV)
2. Joshua came from the Tribe of ______________ and Caleb came from the Tribe of ________________. (Numbers 13:8, see verse 16 and Numbers 13:6, KJV)
3. What were some of the negative comments made by the ten spies who returned from the land of Canaan? (Numbers 13:31-33, KJV)
4. What were some of the positive comments made by Joshua and Caleb concerning the land of Canaan? (Numbers 14:6-8, KJV)
5. What was the fate of the people who murmured and sided with the ten spies? (Numbers 14:26-34, KJV)

Topic: Fasting for the Future

(Esther accepted her destiny)

Scripture Reference: Esther, Chapters 2, 3, 4, and 5

Insight: As humans, one of the hardest things for us to do is practice self-denial.

"Go, gather together all the Jews that are present in Shushan, and fast ye for me, and neither eat nor drink three days, night or day: I also and my maidens will fast likewise; and so will I go in unto the king, which is not according to the law: and if I perish, I perish" Esther 4:16 (KJV).

To many of us, going without food would be considered an imposition. However, fasting allows our focus to be on Jesus, and it is then that we are able to enter into a deeper realm of communication with God.

King Ahasuerus summoned Queen Vashti to his feast so that he could show off her beauty. When the queen refused to appear at the feast, King Ahasuerus became angry. The combination of the king's anger and the convincing counsel of the princes of Persia and Media led to the dethroning of Queen Vashti.

The king issued a decree that all the fair virgins be brought to Shushan. Esther, who had been raised by her uncle, Mordecai, was also brought before the king. Esther had been instructed by Mordecai not to reveal that she was a Jew.

When King Ahasuerus saw Esther, the Scripture says, "And the maiden pleased him, and she obtained kindness of him; and he speedily gave her her things for purification, which such things as

belonged to her, and seven maidens, which were meet to be given her, out of the king's house: and he preferred her and her maids unto the best place of the house of the women"
Esther 2:9 (KJV).

God had given Esther favor before she went before the king. Everyone admired Esther, and when she went before the king, we see God's favor continuing. "And the king loved Esther above all the women, and she obtained grace and favour in his sight more than all the virgins; so that he set the royal crown upon her head, and made her queen instead of Vashti" Esther 2:17 (KJV).

When Haman was promoted by the king, everyone was commanded to reverence Haman. However, Mordecai did not bow to Haman. Mordecai knew that reverence belonged to God and not man. Haman then plotted to destroy Mordecai and all the Jews. Mordecai sent word of Haman's plot to Esther and told her that she would have to go before the king to save her people.

Esther was hesitant and feared death. She sent word back to Mordecai that anyone who went before the king without being requested to appear would die unless the king held out his golden scepter and they were allowed to approach him. Mordecai sent word back to Esther to remind her that although she was queen, she was a Jew first. Mordecai had uncompromising faith. Not only would he not bow down to Haman, but he told Esther that if she did not accept her destiny, that God would save the Jews by other means, but she and her father's house would be destroyed.

Mordecai wanted Esther to know that God did not need her. Esther needed to recognize that there was a reason she had been placed in the position of queen, "and who knoweth whether thou art come the kingdom for such a time as this?" Esther's decision to fast displayed her willingness to trust God and step into her destiny on behalf of her people. Through her fasting, she made her peace with her decision. Through her fasting, she was petitioning God to intervene. She not only fasted, but solicited the cooperation of Mordecai and the Jews at Shushan.

Although Esther had fasted for three days, she did not go before the king feeling weak. She went before the king with boldness and strength. Esther had gained the strength of her conviction as a result of her fast before God. When Esther went before the king, he held out the golden scepter to her and she was allowed to come before him, once again showing that God had granted her favor. "And it was so, when the king saw Esther the queen standing in the court, that she obtained favour in his sight: and the king held out to Esther the golden scepter that was in his hand. So Esther drew near, and touched the top of the scepter" Esther 5:2 (KJV).

Bible Study Questions

1. What happened to Queen Vashti that allowed Esther to become queen? (Esther 1:19, KJV)
2. Who plotted to destroy the Jews? (Esther 3:5-6, KJV)
3. Why did Mordecai have to remind Esther about her heritage? (Esther 4:9-14, KJV)
4. What preparations did Esther make to go before the king on behalf of her people? (Esther 4:15-16, KJV)
5. Do you believe in the power of prayer and fasting? (Personal Reflection)

Topic: How Do You Handle Breaking News?
(God allowed Satan to test Job—an account of Job's trials, paraphrased)
Scripture Reference: Job, Chapter 1 (KJV)

Insight: When we experience tests, the way that we respond demonstrates the level of faith and trust that we have in God.

"And the LORD said unto Satan, Hast thou considered my servant Job, that there is none like him in the earth, a perfect and an upright man, one that feareth God, and escheweth evil?

Then Satan answered the LORD, and said, Doth Job fear God for nought? Hast not thou made an hedge about him, and about his house, and about all that he hath on every side? thou hast blessed the work of his hands, and his substance is increased in the land.

But put forth thine hand now, and touch all that he hath, and he will curse thee to thy face. And the LORD said unto Satan, Behold, all that he hath is in thy power; only upon himself put not forth thine hand. So Satan went forth from the presence of the LORD" Job 1:8-12 (KJV).

Down through the years, many tragic breaking news stories have been reported. The assassination of President John F. Kennedy in 1963 and the assassination of Dr. Martin Luther King Jr. in 1968 were two historic breaking news stories. On September 11, 2001, nearly all the world witnessed the breaking news stories from the U.S. as terrorists hijacked four commercial planes. These hijacked planes were turned into weapons that destroyed thousands of lives, as well as robbing Americans of the perceived security that we once enjoyed. The catastrophic destruction caused by Hurricane Katrina and the broken levees in the city of New Orleans in August of 2005 also managed to capture the attention of the United States and the world. But even before these breaking news stories, there was a breaking news story in the land of Ur.

Imagine with me as Job received breaking news from four reporters. The first reporter began by saying, "Job, we interrupt your life to bring you 'breaking news'!"

"And there came a messenger unto Job, and said, The oxen were plowing, and the asses feeding beside them: And the Sabeans fell upon them, and took them away; yea, they have slain the servants with the edge of the sword; and I only am escaped alone to tell thee" Job 1:14-15 (KJV).

Before that reporter could finish, the second reporter appeared with his news: "The fire of God is fallen from heaven, and hath burned up the sheep, and the servants, and consumed them; and I only am escaped alone to tell thee" Job 1:16b (KJV).

Before Job had an opportunity to reflect on this latest bad news, the third reporter arrived with a news flash: "The Chaldeans made out three bands, and fell upon the camels, and have carried them away, yea, and slain the servants with the edge of the sword; and I only am escaped alone to tell thee" Job 1:17b (KJV).

It seemed that Satan saved the most devastating news for last, as the final reporter entered and delivered his report: "Thy sons and thy daughters were eating and drinking wine in their eldest brother's house: And, behold, there came a great wind from the wilderness, and smote the four corners of the house, and it fell upon the young men, and they are dead; and I only am escaped alone to tell thee" Job 1:18-19 (KJV).

Imagine at that moment, one of Satan's rude reporters sticking a microphone in Job's face and asking one of their favorite questions: "Any comment?"

Job didn't get upset, but responded by saying, "If you will just give me a little time, there is something that I need to do. If you will all come back at around 4pm, I'll hold a news conference about what has happened here today."

The Scripture says, "Then Job arose, and rent his mantle, and shaved his head, and fell down upon the ground, and worshipped" Job 1:20 (KJV). It was not reported that Job lost his temper and yelled at God, or questioned God about the loss of his property or the death of his children. Job did not curse God the way Satan had predicted. Instead, he fell down upon the ground and worshipped.

At 4pm, true to his word, Job held the news conference. He said (paraphrased), "I know you are all here to get your sound bite for the evening news. So I'll give you one statement, and that's it. I won't be taking any questions afterward." Job spoke directly into the microphone. "And said, Naked came I out of my mother's womb, and naked shall I return thither: the LORD gave, and the LORD hath taken away; blessed be the name of the LORD" Job 1:21 (KJV).

It does not matter what breaking news you receive: the death of a loved one, a troubling report from the doctor, a layoff notice from your job, or any other seemingly earth-shattering news; remember that it is only a test. God is still in control. Follow Job's example and fall down and worship God. Pray to God for an answer and the answer will surely come.

Bible Study Questions

1. Why did God recommend Job to Satan? (Job 1:1, KJV)
2. What breaking news did the four messengers bring to Job? (Job 1:14-19, KJV)
3. What was Job's first reaction to all the devastating news he received? (Job 1:20, KJV)
4. What profound statement did Job make regarding his birth and death? (Job 1:21, KJV)
5. When was the last time your received breaking news and how did you react? (Personal Reflection)

Chapter 5: Don't Leave Sound Decision Making on the Pew

Topic: God Changes the Dinner Reservations

(Elijah taught a widow how to set a table)

Scripture Reference: I Kings, Chapter 17:8-16

Insight: God specializes in altering man's plans.

"Elijah said to her, 'Don't be afraid. Go home and do as you have said. But first make a small cake of bread for me from what you have and bring it to me, and then make something for yourself and your son'" I Kings 17:13 (NIV).

The widow of Zarephath was running a race against time and also a race of faith. The widow woman had to make a choice whether to feed her family or to feed a stranger. Her faith race required endurance. The widow felt that she could not finish the race and was about to give up. God sent a track coach by the name of Elijah to encourage her not to stop, but to keep running.

Rao's of New York holds the distinction as the number one spot of the five toughest restaurants to get a reservation in the United States. In a July 13, 2009 article written by Ben Leventhal on the Grub

Street Web site, he compares the experience of making reservations at Rao's to that of securing season tickets. "They're paid for an entire year in advance, so to speak, like season tickets." (Quote does not contain entire sentence.) So I guess it would be safe for us to conclude that our chance of securing a reservation on the same day that we plan to dine is virtually impossible.

There was a drought in the land and therefore no food could be grown. The widow of Zarephath had given careful attention and detail to this last meal that she and her son were about to eat. She had watched her supply of meal and oil closely, and rationed it daily. She knew this day would come, the day of their last meal. Like Rao's, the widow was not accepting any dinner reservations. However, she was not aware that God had plans to send a special dinner guest to her home. She would need to set another place at the table, for now there would be three for dinner.

This was no ordinary guest, but a prophet from God; a prophet who would speak a sustaining word from God. "For thus saith the LORD God of Israel, The barrel of meal shall not waste, neither shall the cruse of oil fail, until the day that the LORD sendeth rain upon the earth" I Kings 17:14 (KJV).

Perhaps the meal and oil would have run out had they come from one of the local merchants. These weren't generic brands, but name brands. The meal and oil came from the Heavenly storehouse and had been manufactured by God. These products were different.

They had sustaining power. Every time the widow thought that the barrel was empty, the meal would still be there. Every time she looked at the oil, it was still there, glistening in the sunlight.

It makes you wonder at what point she realized that the word spoken by the prophet was a word from God that she could depend on. After all, not only had he changed the dinner reservations, but God had also continued to supply the food for the meals on a daily basis. What she had for one day became enough for every day. Her last meal had suddenly become many meals.

Our plans are not God's plans. This widow had planned on cooking her last meal for herself and her son, and then dying. Her plans were changed when Elijah showed up. Now she was cooking for this prophet who told her to cook for him first and then cook for herself and her son. She followed Elijah's instructions, and now there were no more plans for a last meal for two. Instead, there were plans for three diners to eat the next meal and the next meal and the next. The manner in which God performs miracles does not allow man to claim credit.

Bible Study Questions

1. What were the widow's dinner plans before she met Elijah? (I Kings 17:12, KJV)

2. What instructions did she receive from Elijah? (I Kings 17:13, KJV)
3. Why didn't the meal and oil run out? (I Kings 17:14, KJV)
4. Have you ever made a decision out of desperation? (Personal Reflection)
5. Has God ever sent an Elijah to your rescue with tangible results? (Personal Reflection)

Topic: When the Tables Turn
(The rich man needed the beggar, Lazarus)
Scripture Reference: Luke 16:19-31

Insight: We can be in a position of prominence one day and be caught in a downward spiral the next.

"There was a certain rich man, which was clothed in purple and fine linen, and fared sumptuously every day: And there was a certain beggar named Lazarus, which was laid at his gate, full of sores, And desiring to be fed with the crumbs which fell from the rich man's table: moreover the dogs came and licked his sores" Luke 16:19-21 (KJV).

In many major cities, we see people on corners holding up signs: "Will work for food," "Lost job, need help," and other messages. When this activity first started years ago, people would give generously to these helpless individuals. Eventually, the people who really needed help were pushed from their corners and replaced by the people who saw an opportunity to profit by running a good scam.

Lazarus was not running a scam on the rich man. He was evidently the resident beggar for this man's particular gate. Every day that the rich man passed through his gate, he would see Lazarus there. He was aware of Lazarus's presence, but he was not affected by his plight.

The Bible states that Lazarus died and was carried by the angels into Abraham's bosom. The rich man died, and was buried, and in hell, he lifted up his eyes.

The rich man probably did not believe his eyes when he saw Abraham afar off and Lazarus in his bosom. Now we see role reversal at its best. The rich man became the beggar, asking Abraham to allow Lazarus to dip the tip of his finger in water and cool his tongue.

The rich man was no longer concerned about the condition of Lazarus's fingers. These same dirty fingers of a beggar that he once looked down on were now viewed in a different light. He now wanted mercy, but had forgotten that he had never shown mercy. He wanted kindness, but had forgotten that he had never shown kindness. Abraham reminded him that he had enjoyed all the luxuries life had to offer and had not shared them with people in need. He had not acknowledged that God was the one who had blessed him with all that he had. He had already had good things; now, it was Lazarus's turn.

Abraham also let the rich man know that there was another reason his request could not be granted. "And beside all this, between us and you there is a great gulf fixed: so that they which would pass from hence to you cannot; neither can they pass to us, that would come from thence" Luke 16:26 (KJV).

Abraham probably could have told the rich man that this gulf was similar to the gate that that the rich man had put up to keep Lazarus on the outside. The rich man had not stopped at the gate; now, he could not cross the gulf. The rich man had faith in his riches and no faith in God. The devil can guarantee you fifteen minutes of fame on earth, but you may have to spend eternity in hell.

The uncertainties of life dictate that we have to be very careful how we treat people when we are in positions of authority, power, and prestige.

When he was alive, the rich man felt that there was no place for Lazarus on the inside of the gate. Lazarus did not fit in with the rich man's social circle. Lazarus did not have any money, no education, did not come from the right family, so he needed to stay on the outside of the gate. Lazarus was considered as one of the "have-nots"; however, now, Lazarus was on the inside of the gate and in the company of the "haves"—those who have "eternal life."

Bible Study Questions

1. How did the rich man regard life while on earth? (Luke 16:19, KJV)
2. After the rich man and Lazarus the beggar died, where were their final destinations? (Luke 16:22-23, KJV)
3. What did the rich man request of Abraham? (Luke 16:24, KJV)
4. Why couldn't Lazarus help the rich man? (Luke 16:25-26 KJV)
5. Have we become so insensitive to the needs of others that we pass by those in need without a glance? (Personal Reflection)

Topic: "I" Is a Dangerous Letter
(A rich man's solution: build bigger barns)
Scripture Reference: Luke 12:16-20; Proverbs 28:27; Luke 4:18b; John 14:2; Hebrews 11:10; Matthew 16:26

Insight: Many of us are trying to create our own little heavens on earth.

The rich man lived in his man-made heaven filled with possessions that he thought would last forever.

The rich man in this parable felt that he had accomplished everything solely based on his knowledge and expertise. He had no knowledge of Christian charity and it never entered into the appraisal of his situation.

Here he was, faced with making a decision regarding an abundant crop and lack of storage space. Instead of looking at the set of blueprints that Jesus had drawn up for a lasting structure, he chose to demolish the structures that he had and built bigger barns.

Jesus' blueprints offered another option for securing more space. "He that giveth unto the poor shall not lack: but he that hideth his eyes shall have many a curse" Proverbs 28:27 (KJV). Of course, Jesus' floor plans called for plenty of open space, a structure that would be handicapped-accessible so that everyone could enter. In Luke 4:18b, we see a description of this feature: "he hath sent me to heal the brokenhearted, to preach deliverance to the captives, and recovering of sight to the blind, to set at liberty them that are bruised."

The rich man could not bear the thought of sharing any part of his prosperity. He had developed so much wealth that he had created his own little heaven on earth. We see from Luke 12:19 that he was quite content with himself. "And I will say to my soul, Soul, thou hast much goods laid up for many years; take thine ease, eat, drink, and be merry."

Unfortunately, the rich man used faulty building materials when he constructed the bigger barns. He used the wrong brand of materials. He chose "I" lumber, "me" shingles, and "mine" paint. He had no intention of sharing.

He started out with the wrong architect and would not take advantage of the opportunity to correct his mistakes, so his building was not up to code. He didn't bother to look at the work of the greatest architect of all. He should have done as Abraham did in Hebrews 11:10: "For he looked for a city which hath foundations, whose builder and maker is God."

The rich man would discover that his little heaven was temporary and that there was no room for it in God's Heaven. His shabby representation of wealth could not compare with the riches of God. All of the cattle on a thousand hills belong to God. All of the riches of Heaven and Earth belong to God. And what an architect he is. "In my Father's house are many mansions: if it were not so, I would have told you. I go to prepare a place for you" John 14:2 (KJV).

Jesus stated that He came that we might have life and have it more abundantly, but he also stated that he was going away to prepare a place for us, where there would be individual mansions. Wouldn't you agree that that sounds like there is another Heaven in the plans?

The rich man would not live to enjoy his wealth, nor would he have to worry about trying to take his little heaven to God's Heaven. "But God said unto him, Thou fool, this night thy soul shall be required of thee: then whose shall those things be, which thou hast provided?" Luke 12:20 (KJV).

All his wealth would now be enjoyed by others. He was too concerned about his desires to think about his destination. He had not sought the things of God and now his life on earth was ending. "For what is a man profited, if he shall gain the whole world, and lose his own soul? or what shall a man give in exchange for his soul?" Matthew 16:26 (KJV).

When God blesses us with material possessions we should not become consumed with them. Whatever you are making into your little heaven, remember, there is no room for your little heaven in God's Heaven.

Bible Study Questions

1. What did the rich man decide to do when he needed space for his abundant crop? (Luke 12:17-18, KJV)
2. What statement did the rich man make to indicate that he believed his future was secure? (Luke 12:19, KJV)
3. How did God change the rich man's plans? (Luke 12:20, KJV)
4. What statement lets us know that the rich man was really poor? (Luke 12:21, KJV)
5. Are we too focused on our possessions and ourselves? (Personal Reflection)

Topic: You Really Can't Take It with You!
(A young man was faced with a decision)
Scripture Reference: Mark 10:17-27

Insight: The gift of Salvation has already been purchased.

"Then Jesus beholding him loved him, and said unto him, One thing thou lackest: go thy way, sell whatsoever thou hast, and give to the poor, and thou shalt have treasure in heaven: and come, take up the cross, and follow me" Mark 10:21 (KJV).

How many times have you heard the expression "You can't take it with you"? Although we have heard it numerous times, we still have difficulty accepting the fact that when we die, we have to part with our possessions.

When a rich man came to Jesus seeking instructions on how he could obtain eternal life, Jesus' reply caused him to be sorrowful. The man regretted having asked the question because the answer that he received was one that presented him with an unexpected decision. In order to follow Jesus, he had to choose between his riches and Jesus.

He told Jesus that he had kept the commandments from his youth. This may have been admirable, but it would not gain him eternal life. Jesus told him that the one thing that he needed to do was to sell all that he had in order to follow him. This man's faith in his riches led to his failure to follow Jesus.

All the good deeds that we do and the services that we perform cannot be compared to God's righteousness. Salvation is the most precious gift there is and it has to come through Jesus.

Although this incident involved material possessions, many of us are clinging to other things that cause us to misapply our faith. We put our faith in our own abilities, our educational achievements, and our earthly accomplishments. Like this man, we fail to see that although these may be admirable accomplishments, they alone cannot secure eternal life.

A bright-green leaf on a beautiful flower represents life at its best. Unless care and nurturing is given to the plant, the leaves will fade and the flower will eventually die. In some instances, when this deterioration is noticed in time, the life of the plant may be prolonged. But like everything else, with the exception of the Word of God, the plant, which is temporal, will one day pass away.

Have you ever noticed that the flowery words expressed by some speakers at funerals are obvious attempts to lean more toward respectable exaggeration than facts? The flowery words spoken about the character, accomplishments, and prestige of the deceased will fade the same way the beautiful flowers that adorn the altar will fade. We have to plant seeds of obedience to God's word and seeds of service to our fellow man. This is the kind of garden that will yield flowers that can survive in Heaven's atmosphere.

We will not be able to enter Heaven with just our bouquet of "long stem degrees"; they will pale in comparison to the high school dropout's beautiful "bouquet of kindness and charity." We will not be able to enter Heaven with only our lilies of fortune; they will not survive like the homeless person's "arrangement of love." We cannot enter Heaven with just our orchids of fame; though beautiful on earth, they will not compare to the “bouquets of trust in God” that you will see in the hands of a handicapped person or an autistic child.

We have to learn to keep our earthly blessings in perspective. They are temporal. We have to keep our focus on the giver and not the gift. We will not be able to take the gifts with us. We can enjoy the degrees, fortune, and fame that God has blessed us with on earth, but keep them secondary to the blessing of Salvation He has given us, which is eternal.

“It is easier for a camel to go through the eye of a needle, than for a rich man to enter into the kingdom of God” Mark 10:25 (KJV). This is not to say that it is impossible. We know that all things are possible with God. A distinction has to be made regarding the importance of wealth and the willingness to follow Jesus.

Bible Study Questions

1. What question did the rich young ruler asked Jesus about eternal life? (Mark 10:17, KJV)
2. How did the young man respond when Jesus spoke of keeping the commandments? (Mark 10:19-20, KJV)
3. What did Jesus tell the young man that he had to do to have treasures in Heaven? (Mark 10:21, KJV)
4. How did the young man respond to Jesus’ instructions concerning his possessions? (Mark 10:22)

5. Do you put more trust in your material possessions than you do in Jesus? (Personal Reflection)

Chapter 6: Don't Leave Your Knowledge of Miracles on the Pew

Topic: Almost Arrested for Disturbing the Peace

(God breathed life into dried-up bones)

Scripture Reference: Ezekiel, Chapter 37

Insight: We all face "dried-up bones" situations in our lives.

God often spoke to Old Testament prophets through visions. Ezekiel received a vision from God where he was placed in a valley with skeletal remains all around him. In the vision, God asked Ezekiel if the bones could live. Ezekiel's response was that only God knew the answer to that question. "And he said unto me, Son of man, can these bones live? And I answered, O Lord God thou knowest" Ezekiel 37:3 (KJV).

Ezekiel was instructed by God to prophesy to the bones. Ezekiel was to tell the dry bones to hear the word of the Lord that God would breathe life back into them; place flesh back on them and they would once again live. Ezekiel obeyed God and prophesied to the bones. Ezekiel said that while he was prophesying, he witnessed the truth of the prophecy. “So I prophesied as I was commanded: and as I prophesied, there was a noise, and behold a shaking, and the bones came together, bone to his bone” Ezekiel 37:7 (KJV).

Ezekiel was instructed to prophesy to the wind also. “Then he said unto me, Prophesy unto the wind, prophesy, son of man, and say to the wind, Thus saith the Lord God; Come from the four winds, O breath, and breathe upon these slain, that they may live” Ezekiel 37:9 (KJV). Ezekiel said that the bodies came alive and stood up on their feet, representing an exceedingly great army.

What a powerful vision! God used this vision to let Ezekiel know that the bones represented the hopelessness of Israel. God wanted the children of Israel to know that he was able to restore His Spirit in them and give them new life in their own land. “And shall put my spirit in you, and ye shall live, and I shall place you in your own land: then shall ye know that I the Lord have spoken it, and performed it, saith the Lord” Ezekiel 37:14 (KJV).

Many times, we feel like there is no hope. During these times, we are experiencing a spiritual drought in our lives. Our bones may as well be dried up like skeletons. We have no desire to move around. We lie around lifeless and seem to have no energy or desire to do anything. We indulge in pity parties, dig ditches of depression, crawl into holes of hopelessness, and waste time wallowing in wells filled with “What about me?” questions. We spend countless days waiting for our ships to come in. It has never occurred to us that God may be waiting for us to prove that we can handle a ship. Can we set a correct course for a ship and keep it on that course? Can we keep accurate journey logs? Many of us want to be ship captains before we can even demonstrate that we can handle a rowboat.

God has given us his word, which is all the prophecy we need. We need to seek new life through God's word, our prayers, and our praises. We are created as free-willed beings. God is not going to send Ezekiel to ring our doorbell to give us a new prophecy for our dried-up bones. We have already read the vision; it is up to us to seek God for new life. "And whatsoever ye shall ask in my name, that will I do, that the Father may be glorified in the Son. If ye shall ask any thing in my name, I will do it" John 14:13-14 (KJV). Whether the circumstances representing the spiritual droughts in our lives are self-imposed or tests from God, only God can breathe new life into those dead situations.

Bible Study Questions

1. What did God ask Ezekiel about the dry bones? (Ezekiel 37:3, KJV)
2. What happened when Ezekiel first prophesied to the bones? (Ezekiel 37:7, KJV)
3. What happened when Ezekiel prophesied to the wind? (Ezekiel 37:10, KJV)

4. What comparison did God make between the bones and the house of Israel? (Ezekiel 37:11-14, KJV)
5. Is there a dry situation in your life that requires a fresh breath from God? (Personal Reflection)

Topic: Don't Throw Away the Bread Ends
(Jesus fed a multitude)
Scripture Reference: Matthew 14:15-21; John 1:1-2

Insight: God can bless you wherever you are.

"And when it was evening, his disciples came to him, saying, This is a desert place, and the time is now past; send the multitude away, that they may go into the villages, and buy themselves victuals" Matthew 14:15 (KJV).

Jesus had been healing the sick all day, and as the evening was approaching, the disciples came to him to remind him that the people needed to start heading toward the village so that they could buy something to eat for themselves.

Jesus responded to the disciples by telling them that it was not necessary to send the people away. "But Jesus said unto them, They need not depart; give ye them to eat" Matthew 14:16 (KJV). "And they say unto him, we have here but five loaves, and two fishes" Matthew 14:17 (KJV). Before Burger King came up with the Kid's Meal, Jesus took a kid's meal and fed a multitude. Before McDonald's introduced the Happy Meal, Jesus gave out 5,000-plus Happy and Blessed Meals.

"And he commanded the multitude to sit down on the grass, and took the five loaves, and the two fishes, and looking up to heaven, he blessed and brake, and gave the loaves to his disciples, and the disciples to the multitude" Matthew 14:19 (KJV).

First of all, the people had to be correctly positioned. Jesus commanded them to sit down on the grass, which placed them in a position of humility; they were sitting down and looking up to Jesus. Jesus then acknowledged his position as the Son of God by looking to the Father for affirmation as he looked up to Heaven and blessed and broke the bread. The position that the disciples were required to assume was that of servants. He gave the food to his disciples to distribute to the people. We have to be in a position to be blessed and ready to receive the blessing from whatever source or person God chooses to use.

We see four examples of faith in this account of the feeding of the 5,000 plus. First of all, we see the faith of the lad with the lunch. He had faith enough to believe that although he was giving up his lunch, he would not go hungry. Next, we see the faith of the 5,000 plus in their obedience to sit down and wait on the meal. Jesus then displayed faith in the Father as he looked up to heaven and blessed the food. Finally, the disciples showed their faith in Jesus as they took on the roles of servers.

Can you imagine being assigned the task to hand out food to 5,000 people? You might start to worry about what you were going to do after you fed 1,500 and the food ran out; you might worry that a riot might break out because the other 3,500 did not get fed.

But the disciples knew that Jesus was able to provide for the hungry. They remembered the Sabbath day when they were hungry, and following Jesus' lead, they began to pluck the ears of corn and eat. They had not gone hungry since they had been following Jesus. They somehow knew that this miracle-working Jesus would not start something that he could not finish.

And finish it he would, but not like an ordinary man. "And they did all eat, and were filled: and they took up of the fragments that remained twelve baskets full" Matthew 14:20 (KJV). The scripture did not just say they ate, but it said they were filled. So God won't just feed you, he will feed you until you are full. Maybe you just need a small helping to get full or maybe you need more of God. "O taste and see that the Lord is good: blessed is the man that trusteth in him" Psalm 34:8 (KJV).

Even after the crowd had eaten, there were twelve baskets full of fragments. I can imagine that there were some bread ends in the baskets. God specializes in bread ends. Have you ever noticed when you open a loaf of bread that the slices of bread in the middle are really soft? However, the slices won't remain fresh unless you have a bread end at the front of the loaf and at the end of the loaf. "In the beginning was the Word, and the Word was with God, and the Word was God. The same was in the beginning with God" John 1:1-2 (KJV).

When you have finished eating a loaf of bread, what do you do with the bread ends? Some people consider the bread ends as the best part of the bread. I love to make sandwiches with the "ends," as I call them. Other people save them to make bread pudding. But then, others see very little value in them and simply crumble them up and feed them to the birds.

When all the bread in the middle is gone, the two ends are still there. Don't miss out on the best part of the loaf. God provides the bread ends for our lives. God is Alpha and Omega; the beginning and the end. God is the Bread of Life. We don't want to miss out on all that God has for us in the middle of the loaf. That means we have to start out with God and end with God.

Since the bread ends are represented by Alpha and Omega, we have to be very careful because our joy might be in the bread ends, our peace might be in the bread ends, our deliverance might be in the bread ends, our happiness might be in the bread ends, our gifts might be in the bread ends, and our anointing might be in the bread ends. So let us not allow our blessings to be crumbled up and thrown to the birds.

When the evening comes in your life and you find yourself in a desert place, where do you turn? May I suggest that you turn to one who is able to supply the bread ends? God can take impossibilities and turn them into possibilities. Bring your little to God if you need more and watch Him give you much more.

Bible Study Questions

1. How did the lad in this story exemplify faith? (John 6:8-9, KJV)
2. How did Jesus show his faith in God? (Matthew 14:19, KJV)
3. How did the people waiting to be fed exhibit their faith? (Matthew 14:19, KJV)
4. What did the disciples do that proved they had faith in Jesus? (Matthew 14:19, KJV)
5. How many baskets were left after everyone had been fed? (Matthew 14:20, KJV)

Topic: Sight Instead of Silver
(Blind Bartimaeus received his sight)
Scripture Reference: Mark 10:46-52; II Corinthians 5:17, KJV

Insight: Many times, we ask for material blessings when we really need spiritual blessings.

"And Jesus answered and said unto him, What wilt thou that I should do unto thee? The blind man said unto him, Lord, that I might receive my sight" Mark 10:51 (KJV).

What do we know about the blind man who Christ healed? We know that his name was Bartimaeus. He was the son of Timaeus. He sat by the highway, begging, and he was blind! He might have been blind, but there was certainly nothing wrong with his hearing. The Scripture says, "And when he heard that it was Jesus of Nazareth, he began to cry out, and say, Jesus, thou son of David, have mercy on me" Mark 10:47 (KJV).

Consider the blind man's position. He was sitting by the side of the road where people were passing by and dropping coins into whatever container he held out to them. While sitting by the side of the road, he was probably privy to all the news about travelers.

In the past, he had probably listened to the excitement of the crowd when the kings and queens would pass by. He had hoped for and, in many instances, been rewarded by the generosity of this royal entourage. Surely, the kings and queens could be counted on for silver and gold coins.

Yet, the excitement and anticipation that blind Bartimaeus felt when he heard that Jesus would be passing by surpassed the anxiously awaited visits of the kings and queens. The visit from Jesus would mean more than silver and gold. Bartimaeus's sense of hearing was doubly sharp since he did not have his sight. He had heard about this man called Jesus who had walked the coast of Galilee healing the sick and restoring sight to the blind. He had no doubt that Jesus could help him.

Bartimaeus was faced with another challenge. How would he get Jesus to stop? His station in life seemed to be that of a beggar on the side of this highway. Why would Jesus stop to show him mercy? Bartimaeus had no doubt heard that Jesus specialized in helping and healing the downtrodden. Maybe he heard about how Jesus healed the demonic boy or the woman with the issue of blood.

Surely he had heard the travelers talk about how Jesus fed the 5,000 with two small fish and five loaves of bread. How had they approached Jesus for help? How did Jesus become aware of their needs? He had no time to waste on a plan; he simply cried out, "Jesus, thou son of David, have mercy on me" Mark 10:48b.

Bartimaeus knew when to cry out and he knew how to cry out. More importantly, he knew who to cry out to. He knew that what he could get from Jesus was worth crying out for.

Even when the people were telling him to be quiet, he got even louder. No one could imagine what he was going through. Here was an opportunity for him to receive his sight and he was determined that Jesus would hear him that day.

Many times in church services, people will see you stand to your feet and begin praising God, or shouting out, and they are quick to question whether all that is necessary. Be very careful when you judge another person's praise. You don't know what that person has been through. You don't know what they need from God, or what they have already received from God. And for them, yes, it does take all that. In the same way that everyone has their own testimony, everyone has their own expression of praise.

"And Jesus said unto him, Go thy way; thy faith hath made thee whole. And immediately he received his sight, and followed Jesus in the way" Mark 10:52. When Bartimaeus received his sight, he did not go in the other direction. The Scripture says he followed Jesus in the way.

There was no longer a stigma attached to his name. He was no longer referred to as blind Bartimaeus. Think about the stigma that was attached to your name before you met Jesus. You may not want to admit that you had a problem, but the Scripture says that we have all sinned and come short of the Glory of God. Maybe you were known as a liar or a prostitute, a thief or a drug addict, an alcoholic or a gambler, a gossiper or a backstabber, or a hypocrite or backslider.

Before we were saved, we were all spiritually blind. God brought us into the marvelous light. However, many of us still have vision problems. When we became new creatures in Christ, we were given twenty-twenty spiritual vision. "Therefore if any man be in Christ, he is a new creature: old things are passed away; behold all things are become new" II Corinthians 5:17 (KJV).

Remember, if you find yourself doing things that harm your vision, you will not be able to see as clearly. If you frequent dark places and are never exposed to sunlight, you could harm your vision. If you try to read in the dark with very little light, you could harm your vision. If you borrow glasses that were prescribed for someone else, you could harm your vision. Those three previous statements are the kind of statements that preachers make and then say, “You’ll catch that on the way home.”

Be thankful that God has given you twenty-twenty spiritual vision, so that you no longer have to sit by the side of the road, begging for a hand out. You have sight to read God’s Word and learn of his promises. God made us more than conquerors, and as David said, “I have never seen the righteous forsaken nor his seed begging bread.”

Bible Study Questions

1. What did Bartimaeus do when he heard that it was Jesus who was passing by? (Mark 10:47, KJV)
2. What did he do when the people tried to silence him? (Mark 10:48, KJV)
3. What was Bartimaeus’s response to Jesus when asked by Jesus what he wanted of him? (Mark 10:51, KJV)
4. What did Bartimaeus do after he received his sight? (Mark 10:52, KJV)
5. What did you do when you received your spiritual sight as a new creature in Christ? (Personal Reflection)

Topic: A Light at the End of a Water Tunnel
(God was merciful to the children of Israel)

Scripture Reference: Exodus 1:22, Exodus 13:17-22, Exodus Chapter14; Revelation 1:8

Insight: God is a Merciful God and blesses us in spite of our disobedience.

God's hand was on the life of Moses from Moses' birth to his death. The pharaoh issued the order that all of the Hebrew baby boys two years and under were to be thrown into the river. "And Pharaoh charged all his people, saying, Every son that is born ye shall cast into the river, and every daughter ye shall save alive" Exodus 1:22 (KJV).

God used the pharaoh's own daughter to save Moses from death. The pharaoh's daughter pulled Moses from the river and unknowingly sent Moses to be nursed by his own biological mother. Once Moses was returned to the pharaoh's daughter, he was then brought up in the palace as an Egyptian.

When Moses became a man, he witnessed an Egyptian beating a Hebrew. After looking around and thinking that no one saw him, Moses killed the Egyptian and hid him in the sand. Once his action was discovered, Moses had to flee from Egypt to Midian. In Midian, Moses met and eventually married Zipporah.

When God heard the cry of the children of Israel because of their bondage, He chose Moses to lead them out of bondage. After many confrontations with the pharaoh, Moses and the children of

Israel began their exodus in the wilderness. "By day the LORD went ahead of them in a pillar of cloud to guide them on their way and by night in a pillar of fire to give them light, so that they could travel by day or night. Neither the pillar of cloud by day nor the pillar of fire by night left its place in front of the people" Exodus 13:21-22 (NIV).

And the award for inadequate faith by a group goes to the children of Israel. They witnessed God's power during the Passover even before they left Egypt, yet they continued to display inadequate faith.

Being the omniscient God that he is, God knew everything that the children of Israel would need for their exodus from Egypt to the Promised Land. He provided a pillar of cloud as their compass for guidance during the day and a pillar of fire that served as a divine spotlight so that they could travel by night. God positioned an angel who traveled before them with the pillars. God knew that they did not know the way and that they would be fearful at night without light.

God also knew what would happen when they came to the Red Sea. He knew how they would react when they discovered that the pharaoh's soldiers were behind them. They would react in fear and begin to blame Moses for bringing them out of Egypt. God had a divine plan to show them his power and mercy.

Once the Egyptians began to pursue the children of Israel, the pillar of cloud changed position. "And the angel of God, which went before the camp of Israel, removed and went behind them; and the pillar of the cloud went from before their face, and stood behind them: And it came between the camp of the Egyptians and the camp of Israel; and it was a cloud and darkness to them, but it gave light by night to these: so that the one came not near the other all the night" Exodus 14:19-20.

When Moses stretched forth his rod, the waters divided and God caused a strong east wind to blow all night and dry the sea. With the Egyptians behind them and the Red Sea in front of them, the children of Israel were about to enter into a water tunnel of fear. There was a wall of water on the left and a wall of water on the right, but God was providing the light for their walk through the sea.

Once the pharaoh's army entered the water tunnel, God caused the wheels of their chariots to come off. Once they realized that they were up against God, the Egyptians tried to turn around and flee, but God told Moses to stretch out his rod again, and the waters returned to the sea and swallowed up the entire Egyptian army.

Moses was obedient to God and knew that God had provided the dry land as a blessing to the children of Israel. The Egyptians could not operate in that same blessing, because it was not their blessing.

In life, we face problems that seem like water tunnels. We have obstacles to the left and right and the enemy is approaching from the rear. It seems as though there is no light at the end of the tunnel. It is during these times when we have to remember that God is a light at the beginning and at the end of the tunnel. "I am Alpha and Omega, the beginning and the ending, saith the Lord, which is, and which was, and which is to come, the Almighty" Revelation 1:8.

Bible Study Questions

1. How was God's hand on Moses when he was a baby? (Exodus 2:10, KJV)
2. What assignment did God have for Moses? (Exodus 3:7-10, KJV)
3. After Moses began the exodus with the children of Israel, what was one of the first major challenges they faced? (Exodus 14:10, KJV)
4. How did God provide safe passage for them to cross the Red Sea? (Exodus 14:21-22, KJV)
5. Are you able to recognize the hand of God working in your life? (Personal Reflection)

Chapter 7: Don't Leave Perseverance on the Pew

Topic: No Melody at Marah

(The children of Israel lacked perseverance)

Scripture Reference: Exodus 15:22-24; Revelation 1:8

Insight: One day, you may see a rainbow after a storm, and the next day, you may see another storm.

"And when they came to Marah, they could not drink of the waters of Marah, for they were bitter: therefore the name of it was called Marah" Exodus 15:23 (KJV).

There are very few people who have not heard the story of Moses stretching forth his rod and the waters of the Red Sea parting, allowing the children of Israel to cross over on dry land. Even those who have not read the Bible story have seen the movie version, *The Ten Commandments*, and perhaps even misguidedly believe that actor Charlton Heston was actually the one who held out the rod and not Moses.

Whatever the case may be, it is a familiar story. For many, the story ends there. Of course, as Christians, we know that it was definitely not the case. It was not a fairy tale where everyone lived happily ever after.

As the children of Israel were safely on dry land and watched as the pharaoh's army drowned, the Scripture says that Miriam and her choir members began to sing praises, glorifying God. After this celebration, they headed toward the wilderness of Shur. They went for three days without water until they came to Marah, where they found water. But just as Miriam was about to pull out the tambourine and tell the choir members to take the stand, something happened. They discovered that the water was not fit to drink because it was bitter.

How many times have you thought you were about to come out of a situation and just when you were about to praise God, you found out that things had not really turned out the way you expected? Did you make the same mistake as Miriam and put away the tambourine? Did you find yourself like the people on that TV show, *Don't Forget the Lyrics!*? Did you forget the words to your praise song?

Let's not be too hard on the children of Israel, because when we come to the Marahs in our lives, we, too, forget the lyrics. We may not be in Egypt under a pharaoh, but there are Egypts from which we are trying to escape. And when God brings us out of Egypt and crosses us over those obstacles, sometimes we find ourselves at Marah. If you have never faced a Marah, just keep on living.

You may be trying to escape from an Egypt of financial uncertainty, or an Egypt of loneliness, sickness, or grief. You may find yourself in an Egypt without peace or joy. As we reside here on earth as pilgrims traveling through, we must realize that while there is secured salvation through faith, we are not promised immunity from problems.

In July of 2009, I visited my ninety-year-old father in Louisiana and we had one of the best visits we have ever had. He was proud to show off the rows of mustard greens that he had planted and I was happy that he was still able to do what he loved. In September of 2009, my father was diagnosed with kidney failure, and on December 26, 2009, he passed away. Now I found myself at "Marah" and the water was bitter.

I spent many hours on my knees and had to go deep into God's word to get through my Marah. The key is that you have to come through praising God. I discovered that the one thing that allows you to keep singing a melody at Marah is to remember who God is. Circumstances and situations may change, but God never changes. "'I am the Alpha and the Omega,' says the Lord God, 'who is, and who was, and who is to come, the Almighty'" Revelation 1:8 (NIV).

Bible Study Questions

1. How many days did the people look for water in the wilderness of Shur? (Exodus 15:22, KJV)
2. What happened when they found water in Marah? (Exodus 15:23, KJV)
3. What was the people's attitude toward Moses concerning the waters at Marah? (Exodus 15:14, KJV)
4. What instructions did Moses follow from God to make the waters at Marah sweet? (Exodus 15:25, KJV)
5. Have you ever celebrated a breakthrough only to discover that you are at Marah facing bitter waters? (Personal Reflection)

Topic: What Is Your Shelf Life?
(Jeremiah visited the potter's house)
Scripture Reference: Jeremiah 18:1-6

Insight: Only God can reshape brokenness and create perfect vessels.

"O house of Israel, cannot I do with you as this potter? saith the Lord. Behold, as the clay is in the potter's hand, so are ye in mine hand, O house of Israel" Jeremiah 18:6 (KJV).

Jeremiah was instructed by God to go to the potter's house and observe the potter as he worked with the clay. "The word which came to Jeremiah from the LORD, saying, Arise, and go down to the potter's house, and there I will cause thee to hear my words. Then I went down to the potter's house, and, behold, he wrought a work on the wheels" Jeremiah 18:1-3 (KJV). By observing the potter, Jeremiah would be able to let the nation of Israel know that God was in control of their lives.

When this parable is discussed, a lot of emphasis is placed on the work of the potter as he formed the vessel. We should also examine the process that takes place after the vessel is formed. During Bible times, the potter would use a small piece of wood to smooth the outside of the vessel. Once the potter had finished the vessel and it met his specifications, he would place it on the shelf until it was set.

The potter would examine the vessel carefully to ensure that it had been on the shelf for the appropriate amount of time. If the vessel was placed in the oven too soon, it could not withstand the fire and would crack. Once the potter determined that the vessel was ready for the oven, it would be placed into the oven so that it could be strengthened by the fire.

God sent Jesus to earth to experience the trials and tribulations that man would encounter. This act represented the potter working with the clay to get the right consistency. Since Jesus knew all about the rough edges of our lives, He knew just how to administer each individual smoothing process.

The Cross of Calvary represents the potter's shelf. Only a perfect vessel could be put on the shelf of Calvary. Only a perfect vessel could remain there long enough to be ready to go through the fire of death and pay the price for man's sins. That vessel was Jesus. Jesus could have come down from the cross, but he remained there because of the love that he has for you and me.

Today, we buy food in containers, and once the jars or packages are opened, some of them require refrigeration. We also purchase food items in cans and boxes that we place on our pantry shelves. These products last longer and are referred to as having shelf life. There are expiration dates marked on the cans and boxes. The expirations dates on the pantry items can extend up to a year or sometimes longer, depending on the product, but none of them lasts forever.

As mere mortals, we, too, have expiration dates. The only way that we can get to the Heavenly storehouse and experience eternal shelf life is to allow our lives to be shaped by God, the greatest potter of all.

Bible Study Questions

1. Why did God send Jeremiah to watch the potter work? (Jeremiah 18:1, KJV)
2. What did the potter do with the marred vessel? (Jeremiah, 18:4, KJV)
3. What did God want Jeremiah to tell the children of Israel? (Jeremiah 18:11, KJV)

4. Do you realize that we were all broken vessels once? (Personal Reflection)
5. Do we really want God to mold us and make us after His will? (Personal Reflection)

Topic: A Positive ID

(John sent two disciples to look for Jesus)

Scripture Reference: Matthew 11:2-11; Ephesians 3:16-17

Insight: Faith provides surety of God's existence in our lives.

John, known as John the Baptist, was in prison and was desperate to find out if the man he had been hearing about was really Christ. When you are really seeking answers, sometimes you may have to rely on others to help you. However, unlike John, we have been blessed with the Word of God and the freedom to explore that Word, wherein lies the truth.

"Now when John had heard in the prison the works of Christ, he sent two of his disciples, And said unto him, Art thou he that should come, or do we look for another?" Matthew 11:2-3 (KJV).

It is unfortunate that in our society today, many couples anticipating marriage feel the need to secure the services of a private investigator. Instead of deciding where to set up their wedding registry, they are looking for someone to investigate the person they are considering marrying. They want to know if the person they are thinking about committing the rest of their life to is indeed the person he or she professes to be. The job of the investigator is to look into the person's background as well as present activities. The investigator will bring back documents and pictures as proof that the individual is or is not involved in unscrupulous activities.

John was not trying to find out about unscrupulous activities. He wanted confirmation of the good news that he had heard of the wonderful miracles that Jesus was performing. Being in prison, John was in no position to find out on his own if this was Christ. John wanted to know if this was indeed the Christ, the one he had committed his life to, the one he had told so many others about; the one whose doctrine he had gone to prison for and was about to die for. John sent two of his disciples, certainly men he trusted, to go and ask Jesus if he was the "one," or if they should look for another.

When asked the question, "Jesus answered and said unto them, Go and shew John again those things which ye do hear and see: The blind receive their sight, and the lame walk, the lepers are cleansed, and the deaf hear, the dead are raised up, and the poor have the gospel preached to them. And blessed is he, whosoever shall not be offended in me" Matthew 11:4-6 (KJV). This was the proof that John needed to make a positive ID. The Word had sent the Word back to him, which was as sound as any fingerprint or DNA test result.

Jesus was truly the one who had come to bear the sins of the world. Jesus acknowledged to the crowd that John was considered by him to be more than a prophet. “Verily I say unto you, Among them that are born of women there hath not risen a greater than John the Baptist: notwithstanding he that is least in the kingdom of heaven is greater than he” Matthew 11:11 (KJV). When we are seeking Jesus, we can refer to Paul’s prayer in Ephesians. “That he would grant you, according to the riches of his glory, to be strengthened with might by his Spirit in the inner man; That Christ may dwell in your hearts by faith; that ye, being rooted and grounded in love, May be able to comprehend with all saints what is the breadth, and length, and depth, and height; And to know the love of Christ, which passeth knowledge, that ye might be filled with all the fulness of God” Ephesians 3:16-19 (KJV).

Bible Study Questions

1. Where was John when he heard about the works of Christ? (Matthew 11:2, KJV)
2. How many of his disciples did he send to search for Jesus? (Matthew 11:2, KJV)
3. What question did John’s disciples ask Jesus? (Matthew 11:3, KJV)
4. What message did Jesus send back to John by the disciples? (Matthew 11:4-6, KJV)
5. What did Jesus tell the crowd about John? (Matthew 11:11, KJV)

Topic: Does Anyone Really Have Your Back?
(Aaron and Hur supported Moses)
Scripture Reference: Exodus 17: 8-12

Insight: God is the only consistent and reliable resource that never fails.

It has become more of a cliché when someone says, “I’ve got your back,” and it no longer carries the intensity of a promise. Being able to count on people for support is slowly becoming obsolete and can be found archived with other morally obligatory actions that were once a major part of our lives.

The Israelites once again found themselves engaged in battle. This time, their enemy was Amalek. Moses had faith that God would allow them to prevail against Amalek.

The rod that God had given Moses would prove to be the symbol of victory in this battle. The lifting of the rod during the battle would ensure that the Lord was with them in the battle. The Israelites had already witnessed the power that God had demonstrated through the rod that Moses carried. And as they went into battle against Amalek, the rod would play another important role.

“And Moses said unto Joshua, Choose us out men, and go out, fight with Amalek: tomorrow I will stand on the top of the hill with the rod of God in mine hand” Exodus 17:9 (KJV). Moses instructed Joshua to choose men to fight against Amalek, and he (Moses), along with Aaron and Hur, would go to the top of the hill. Once at the top of the hill, Moses would lift up the rod of God. Aaron and Hur were with Moses to offer physical support. However, God would provide the ultimate strength.

God knew that Moses would not be able to stand at the top of the hill and hold the rod up throughout the entire battle. "So Joshua did as Moses had said to him, and fought with Amalek: and Moses, Aaron, and Hur went up to the top of the hill. And it came to pass, when Moses held up his hand, that Israel prevailed: and when he let down his hand, Amalek prevailed" Exodus 17:10-11 (KJV).

As the battle continued, Moses' hands became tired and he found it very difficult to hold the rod in place. "But Moses' hands were heavy; and they took a stone, and put it under him, and he sat thereon; and Aaron and Hur stayed up his hands, the one on the one side, and the other on the other side; and his hands were steady until the going down of the sun" Exodus 17:12 (KJV). There is a key point in verse 12, where Aaron and Hur slid a stone under Moses so that he could sit down and continue to hold on to the rod. This act signifies that Aaron and Hur respected the authority that God had given to Moses. They did not take the rod from Moses when they saw that he was becoming weary.

They realized that if the rod were taken out of the hands of Moses, it would become as any other stick they might find by the riverbank. The assignment of holding up the rod belonged to Moses.

They had been assigned to offer physical support to Moses. It is so important to have friends who recognize our weaknesses, yet also recognize and appreciate our strengths.

Moses displayed uncompromising faith that God would empower him through the rod, and he knew how important it was to keep the rod lifted up. Aaron and Hur believed that Moses had been chosen by God and had faith in the action that Moses was undertaking. Once they slid the stone under Moses, the Scripture says that "his hands were steady until the going down of the sun."

Are you trying to balance the weight of your problems on a rod that has not been issued to you by God? Are you accepting help from the right people? You have to be very careful when you accept help from sources that are not sanctioned by God. It becomes extremely hard to focus and keep things in perspective when you are weary and unable to think straight.

Many times in our lives, our situations seem unbearable. Those are the times when our hands are getting heavy. Before we reach the point where it seems like we are about to drop the rod and lose the battle, God will send an Aaron and Hur into our lives who will slide a rock under us so we can sit down and reevaluate the situation.

A rock is a solid object that offers stability. When God sends Aaron and Hur with our rocks, they are being sent to point us in the direction of God. True friends who will stick with you in the real battles are difficult to find. Pray to God so that you will be able to recognize your Aaron and Hur. Sometimes, when the trials of this life have us down, we do not think about looking up. But if we will just look up toward Heaven and reach out to God in prayer, we will discover that God is always looking down to see about us.

Bible Study Questions

1. What instructions did Moses give to Joshua concerning the battle of Amalek? (Exodus 17:9, KJV)
2. Who accompanied Moses up the hill? (Exodus 17:10, KJV)
3. What part did Moses' rod play in the battle? (Exodus 17:11, KJV)
4. What happened when Moses became too tired to hold up the rod? (Exodus 17:12, KJV)
5. Do you have friends you can count on like Aaron and Hur? (Personal Reflection)

Chapter 8: Don't Leave Obedience on the Pew

Topic: The Portfolio of a Peacemaker

(Abram settled a dispute between herdsmen)

Scripture Reference: Genesis, Chapter 13; Matthew 5:9; Hebrews 12:13

Insight: It is easy to react to a difficult situation in anger, but with God's guidance, peace will prevail.

"And the land was not able to bear them, that they might dwell together: for their substance was great, so that they could not dwell together" Genesis13:6 (KJV).

A peacemaker is often called on to be the one who gives up what is right in order to keep peace. The Scripture tells us, "Blessed are the peacemakers: for they shall be called the children of God" Matthew 5:9 (KJV).

Abram was certainly a child of God, and he was called on to be a peacemaker. When Abram began his journey from his homeland, his nephew, Lot, came along with him. Abram had been sent by the hand of God. I've heard preachers say that Lot raised his own hand and volunteered for the journey.

"And Abram was very rich in cattle, in silver and in gold" Genesis 13:2 (KJV). Lot also had flocks, herds, and tents. When bickering and strife broke out between Abram's and Lot's herdsmen, Abram realized that in order for him and his nephew to maintain a harmonious relationship, they would have to part ways. "Is not the whole land before thee? separate thyself, I pray thee, from me: if thou wilt take the left hand, then I will go to the right; or if thou depart to the right hand, then I will go to the left" Genesis 13:9 (KJV).

Abram, being the elder member of the family, did not have to give Lot a choice as to where he should pitch his tents. However, many times, wise judgment is the better choice when trying to diffuse a challenging situation. In some instances, one might consider using strong tactics, hoping to end the situation by exercising seniority, when in reality, instead of extinguishing the fire, you simply create other smoldering embers that will eventually refuel the fire.

Abram avoided this possibly explosive situation by approaching it diplomatically. He not only gave Lot a choice, but he gave him first choice. At first glance, it might be concluded that Lot took advantage of Abram.

"And Lot lifted up his eyes, and beheld all the plain of Jordan, that it was well watered everywhere, before the Lord destroyed Sodom and Gomorrah, even as the garden of the Lord, like the land of Egypt, as thou comest unto Zoar. Then Lot chose him all the plain of Jordan;

and Lot journeyed east: and they separated themselves the one from the other" Genesis 13:10-11 (KJV).

Abram had the greater advantage, because he had God on his side. Abram knew that God would be with him in whatever land he chose to dwell. Abram had uncompromising faith in God. God made Abram a promise after Lot left: "And the LORD said unto Abram, after that Lot was separated from him, Lift up now thine eyes, and look from the place where thou art northward, and southward, and eastward, and westward: For all the land which thou seest, to thee will I give it, and to thy seed for ever" Genesis 13:14-15 (KJV).

It is important to note that God spoke to Abram after Lot headed east. Many times, God does not bless us until we separate ourselves from people who are not in His will. These people may be hindering us from being completely in God's will.

As Christians, our very nature should be that of a peacemaker. If the Holy Spirit dwells within us, then that Spirit is able to empower us to be at peace with all men. "Follow peace with all men, and holiness, without which no man shall see the Lord" Hebrews 12:14 (KJV). Being a peacemaker does not indicate weakness, but it shows that your character is much stronger than the other person involved in the conflict.

Bible Study Questions

1. What happened when Abram and Lot became prosperous? (Genesis 13:2-5, KJV)
2. What solution did Abram offer to Lot to try and bring peace between the two of them and their herdsmen? (Genesis 13:9-10, KJV)
3. Why was Abram content to give Lot first choice of the land? (Genesis 12:1-3, KJV)
4. What did God promise Abram after Lot went away? (Genesis 13:14-17, KJV)
5. Is someone in your life blocking your blessings? (Personal Reflection)

Topic: No DNA Test Required
(Joseph received a visit from an angel)
Scripture Reference: Matthew 1:18-25; Luke 1:28, 35, 37

Insight: Making hasty decisions often causes us to miss out on blessings.

"But while he thought on these things, behold, the angel of the LORD appeared unto him in a dream, saying, Joseph, thou son of David, fear not to take unto thee Mary thy wife: for that which is conceived in her is of the Holy Ghost. And she shall bring forth a son, and thou shalt call his name JESUS: for he shall save his people from their sins" Matthew 1:20-21.

Many times, we struggle with accepting God's will. When we begin to question the will of God for our lives, we need to look at the engagement of Joseph and Mary.

Was there anyone who should have had more questions than Joseph? Engaged to Mary, whom he believed to be a virgin, he was now faced with making a decision that would change his life forever.

"And the angel answered and said unto her, The Holy Ghost shall come upon thee, and the power of the Highest shall overshadow thee: therefore also that holy thing which shall be born of thee shall be called the Son of God" Luke 1:35 (KJV).

Can you imagine what joy and exuberance Mary felt after she got over the initial shock of Angel Gabriel's visit? Of course, Mary had concerns. How could she give birth to a child when she had never been with a man?

Mary was probably the first person to consider what effect this would have on Joseph. Would he believe her when she told him that she had been favored to give birth to the Son of God? Would he break off their engagement?

There were so many things to consider, yet the fact that she was blessed and highly favored outweighed the negative considerations. "And the angel came in unto her, and said, Hail, thou that art highly favoured, the Lord is with thee: blessed art thou among women" Luke 1:28. She, Mary, a poor peasant girl, had been chosen from among all women to give birth to Jesus. Mary was consoled by the promise, "For with God nothing shall be impossible" Luke 1:37.

Can you imagine the thoughts that were going through Joseph's mind? What would people say? Had Mary been unfaithful? What should he do? Who could he ask for advice? Joseph decided that he would break off their engagement privately to save Mary from any public humiliation.

Before Joseph could carry out his plan, God's will was revealed to him. Any concerns or fears that Joseph had were dissolved after hearing from the angel of God. This revelation strengthened Joseph's love for Mary and allowed them to endure a future filled with whisperers and gossipers. Mary and Joseph trusted in the word they received from God and were able to endure the speculations of doubters.

DNA testing was first established in 1985 by Sir Alec Jeffreys, and it is used for identification purposes as well as determining paternity. DNA is copied from generation to generation, from parents to children. If DNA testing had been in existence during the time of Mary and Joseph, perhaps Joseph would have been encouraged by others to request a DNA test. After all, there were rumors being spread about whether or not Joseph was the father of Mary's baby.

DNA or **d**eoxyribo**n**ucleic **a**cid testing on Jesus would have confused even the most brilliant scientists. Both Joseph and Mary received confirmation from God that Mary would conceive a child because she had been overshadowed by the power of the Holy Ghost. Mary and Joseph performed the duties of earthly parents and raised Jesus as their son, but they would be blessed to become joint heirs with the Son of God.

As Christians, when we consider the acronym DNA as related to Jesus, the results should always show: D = Divine Deliverer, N = Need Supplier, and A = Almighty and Always in Authority.

Bible Study Questions

1. What news did the Angel of the Lord bring to Mary? (Luke 1:30-33, KJV)
2. What question did Mary have for the Angel? (Luke 1:34, KJV)
3. What was Joseph's initial reaction to Mary's news? (Matthew 1:19, KJV)
4. How was Joseph's plan to end his engagement to Mary changed? (Matthew 1:20-21, KJV)
5. What was the saying from the prophet concerning Jesus' birth? (Matthew 1:22-23, KJV)

Topic: The Cure for a Superiority Complex

(Peter and Cornelius had visions)

Scripture Reference: Acts 10:1-35; Acts 11:18

Insight: We are all the same in God's sight; therefore, we cannot justify looking down on anyone.

Have you ever been accused of having the Big Head disorder? One of the symptoms of the Big Head disorder is related to superiority. When the word superior is used in relationship to human beings, it is in direct contrast to humility. I am not sure which word I despise more, boss or superior. As a child of God, I do not feel inferior to any other human being. That is not to say that you should not respect people who are in positions of authority, but you are not supposed to reverence or worship them. God is the only one who is to be revered and worshipped.

"And as Peter was coming in, Cornelius met him, and fell down at his feet, and worshipped him. But Peter took him up, saying, Stand up; I myself also am a man" Acts 10:25-26 (KJV).

Cornelius was a devout man who prayed to God and shared his wealth with the people. The angel of God appeared to Cornelius in a dream, telling him that God had recognized his prayers and his generosity. He was instructed to send men to Joppa and have them contact Peter, and once Peter arrived, he would tell Cornelius what he needed to do.

The next day, after the angel of the Lord had appeared to Cornelius, the men began their journey to Joppa in search of Peter. As the men drew near to Joppa, Peter went up to the rooftop to pray. While on the rooftop, Peter became very hungry. While he waited for the food to be prepared, he fell into a trance. While in the trance, he saw heaven open up and saw a vessel coming down that looked like a great sheet knit at four corners, and it was let down to the earth.

The Scripture details the vessel's contents and Peter's reaction: "Wherein were all manner of fourfooted beasts of the earth, and wild beasts, and creeping things, and fowls of the air. And there came a voice to him, Rise, Peter; kill, and eat. But Peter said, Not so, Lord; for I have never eaten anything that is common or unclean. And the voice spake unto him again the second time, What God hath cleansed, that call not thou common" Acts 10:12-15 (KJV).

This was shown to Peter three times, and then the vessel was received up again into heaven. Before Peter had time to figure out what this vision meant, the men sent by Cornelius had arrived and Peter was told by the Spirit that three men were there looking for him. He was told by the Spirit not to doubt anything, just to go with them because the Spirit had sent them.

"And as Peter was coming in, Cornelius met him, and fell down at his feet, and worshipped him. But Peter took him up, saying, Stand up; I myself also am a man" Acts 10:25-26 (KJV). Peter admonished him to stand up because he himself was only a man. Peter was a Jew, and according to the law, he was not to keep company with people of other nationalities. He reminded Cornelius of this law and informed him that the only reason he was there was because God had shown him that he was not to call common or unclean what God had cleansed. So Peter obeyed God and was at the home of Cornelius. Cornelius informed Peter of his vision and how God wanted him to send for Peter because Peter would bring a word from God.

Once Peter heard about Cornelius's vision, he then began to understand his own experience. "Then Peter opened his mouth, and said, Of a truth I perceive that God is no respecter of persons: But in every nation he that feareth him, and worketh righteousness, is accepted with him. The word which God sent unto the children of Israel, preaching peace by Jesus Christ: (he is Lord of all:)" Acts 10:34-36.

Peter then preached the gospel of the resurrection of Jesus, and while he was preaching, Cornelius and all of the people who were there received the Holy Ghost. Of course, when the apostles and the brethren in Judea heard about Peter's visit to the house of Cornelius, they questioned his actions. Once Peter explained his vision to them, they realized their own flawed judgment. "When they heard these things, they held their peace, and glorified God, saying, Then hath God also to the Gentiles granted repentance unto life" Acts 11:18 (KJV).

Bible Study Questions

1. Why Did Cornelius send for Peter? (Acts 10:1-6, KJV)
2. What was Peter doing when he experienced his vision? (Acts 10:9-10, KJV)

3. What lesson did Peter learn about God from his vision? (Acts 10:28, KJV)
4. What did Peter learn from his visit to Cornelius? (Acts 10:34-36, KJV)
5. What happened when Peter preached about Jesus? (Acts 10:39-44, KJV)

Topic: We Are Not Calling Him Junior!

(Zechariah followed God's instructions)

Scripture Reference: Luke, Chapter 1

Insight: Never doubt God's instructions or delay obedience to his word.

"And he asked for a writing table, and wrote, saying, His name is John. And they marvelled all" Luke 1:63 (KJV).

Years ago, expectant parents trying to decide on baby names purchased books specifically devoted to helping them choose just the right name. Now, with the introduction of the Internet, most parents search for names online. The Web site nameberry.com boasts of a comprehensive database of baby names and displays the top 100 most popular names in the US for baby girls and baby boys from year to year. For the year 2012, the name "John" ranked number 28 on the list for baby boy names, with the name "Jacob" receiving the number one spot.

However, as far as Zacharias and Elisabeth were concerned, "John" was number one on their list because God instructed them that their baby boy would be called "John." Zacharias went into the temple to perform his duties as a priest and burn incense on the altar. While performing his duties, the angel of the Lord appeared to him and he became afraid. "But the angel said unto him, Fear not, Zacharias: for thy prayer is heard; and thy wife Elisabeth shall bear thee a son, and thou shalt call his name John" Luke1:13 (KJV).

After the angel described how John would do great things and bring many to Christ, Zacharias began to question the logic of such a birth. "And the angel answering said unto him, I am Gabriel, that stand in the presence of God; and am sent to speak unto thee, and to shew thee these glad tidings. And, behold, thou shalt be dumb, and not able to speak, until the day that these things shall be performed, because thou believest not my words, which shall be fulfilled in their season" Luke1:19-20 (KJV).

First of all, Gabriel wanted Zacharias to know that he was not just a rank-and-file angel, but an angel who stood in the presence of God. Could it have been that God had given Gabriel instructions to strike Zacharias dumb if he doubted the message, or was Gabriel authorized to make this decision?

Once Zacharias came out of the temple, the people thought that maybe he had seen a vision and could not speak. Many times, when we doubt God's word, we experience a season of silence when it seems like we can't hear from God. During this time, God is allowing us to experience the consequences of not trusting Him.

After Elisabeth gave birth, eight days later, the baby was circumcised according to the custom, and everyone called the baby Zacharias. Elisabeth had to correct them: "And his mother answered and said, Not so; but he shall be called John" Luke 1:60 (KJV). Of course, their relatives could not understand her choice of names because no one in her family was named John. At this time, the word spoken by the angel Gabriel was about to come to fruition. No doubt everyone wanted to see Zacharias's reaction to Elisabeth's choice of a name. After Zacharias confirmed in writing that the baby would be called John, Zacharias's obedience was rewarded. "And his mouth was opened immediately, and his tongue loosed, and he spake, and praised God" Luke 1:64.

Although Zacharias's doubt caused him to endure silence, his obedience resulted in his voice being returned to him and praises to God being uttered from his mouth.

Bible Study Questions

1. Who did God send to announce John's birth to Zacharias? (Luke 1:19, KJV)
2. How was Zacharias punished for doubting God's message? (Luke 1:20, KJV)
3. How many months did Elisabeth hide the fact that she had conceived? (Luke 1:24-25, KJV)

4. What happened when Mary visited Elisabeth? (Luke 1:39-42, KJV)
5. How was Zacharias able to regain his speech? (Luke 1:59-64, KJV)

Chapter 9: Don't Leave Your Knowledge of God's Power on the Pew

Topic: A Faith that Reversed Protocol

(A Canaanite woman's daughter was healed)

Scripture Reference: Matthew 15:21-28; Luke 14:11

Insight: In life, sometimes the right choice is not to accept the finality of a situation.

Protocol plays an important part in formal dinners. From the RSVP invitations to the seating arrangements, place cards, correct table settings, and toasts, no details are left to chance. Jewish traditions and customs dictated that protocol be observed during Bible times. A woman of Canaan asked Jesus to heal her daughter who was vexed with a devil. Although the disciples tried to send her away, her faith made her press ahead boldly.

When Jesus responded to the woman's request that her daughter be healed, He admonished her to remember that the requests for healing from the children of the house of Israel would take precedence over her request.

Jesus used the analogy of the children being fed first before the dogs were fed. "He replied, 'It is not right to take the children's bread and toss it to their dogs.' 'Yes, Lord,' she said, 'but even the dogs eat the crumbs that fall from their masters' table'" Matthew 15:26-27 (NIV).

The woman boldly told Jesus that the dogs, too, needed to be fed, and if they were willing to accept the crumbs from the table, they should not be denied. The woman's argument was that by responding to her need, Jesus would not be depriving the children of Israel of their blessings. The woman's reply might have appeared to be bold; however, it was bolstered by her faith and also tempered with humility. "For whosoever exalteth himself shall be abased; and he that humbleth himself shall be exalted" Luke 14:11.

The woman's faith suggested that she didn't want to take a lot of the Master's time; she just needed a crumb. She didn't want to take anyone else's seat at the table; just let her catch a crumb from the table.

She knew that her name was not on any of the place cards; she just needed a crumb. She knew she didn't belong to the house of Israel; she just needed a crumb. She wasn't there to be seen by the crowd of sophisticated people; she just needed a crumb. She was unselfishly seeking a crumb of healing for her daughter.

Jesus recognized that this woman had unwavering faith. She would not be intimidated by the disciples. Jesus' words to her were challenging, yet she did not relent in her quest to secure a healing for her daughter. This kind of faith could not go unrewarded. "Then Jesus answered and said unto her, O woman, great is thy faith: be it unto thee even as thou wilt. And her daughter was made whole from that very hour" Matthew 15:28.

Bible Study Questions

1. Why was the woman of Canaan coming to Jesus? (Matthew 15:22 KJV)
2. How did the disciples react to the woman? (Matthew 15: 23 KJV)
3. What was Jesus' response to the woman's request? (Matthew 15:25-26 KJV)
4. What statement did the woman make that demonstrated humility? (Matthew 15:27 KJV)
5. Why do you think Jesus' granted this woman's request? (Matthew 15:28 KJV)

Topic: A Prescription with Unlimited Refills
(Paul asked God to remove a thorn)
Scripture Reference: II Corinthians 12:1-10; I Peter 5:10-11

Insight: God knows how to bless us, when to bless us, where to bless us, and what to bless us with.

"For this thing I besought the Lord thrice, that it might depart from me" II Corinthians 12:8 (KJV).

In the twelfth chapter of Corinthians, Paul spoke of having a vision where he went up to the third Heaven and heard things that mortals are not allowed to hear. Was Paul describing being in the presence of God? There are numerous debates regarding Paul's vision as well as his reference to the thorn in his flesh.

Paul did not want to boast about being permitted to go to Paradise, and just in case he would begin to think too highly of himself, he was given a thorn in his flesh as a reminder that he was human and would endure suffering and pain. The debate arises as to whether this was physical pain or mental stress. Whether it was a physical affliction that was obvious to the human eye or whether it was a mental condition that caused him depression and anxiety, we do not know. However, this thorn could be described as a thorn of humility.

Paul could not do anything on his own and God could not use him if he had any thoughts that he (Paul) had any power of his own. There is no doubt that God could have removed the thorn if he so desired. Like all great surgeons, God is not going to perform a surgical procedure if it is not necessary.

By the time a surgeon has become known as a great surgeon, he does not need to perform surgery based on monetary compensation only or to gain notoriety or to enhance his own ego. Before a great surgeon will even consider taking on a patient who he is not already treating, it has to be a case referral. The case has to be in his particular field of expertise, representing unusual circumstances, and also, all other options by that patient's current physician have been exhausted.

Paul could not wait for a referral, so he went straight to God and asked that the thorn be removed.

In response to Paul's first request, God would not even give him an appointment. Paul went to God the second time and asked that the thorn be removed. God took a look at the X-rays, but told Paul that he would not remove it. When Paul went back to God the third time, God wrote Paul a prescription for "Sufficient Grace." It was as though God told Paul to take one capsule daily until God's strength was made perfect in Paul's weakness. "And he said unto me, My grace is sufficient for thee: for my strength is made perfect in weakness. Most gladly therefore will I rather glory in my infirmities, that the power of Christ may rest upon me" II Corinthians 12:9 (KJV).

When God writes you a prescription, you don't have to worry about whether you should get the generic brand or the name brand, whether it is covered by Medicare or your HMO plan. God does not write prescriptions that he cannot fill. Paul did not realize that each time he went to God, he was being dispensed a dosage of Grace.

You may feel that there is a thorn in your life that you have been praying to God to remove. Don't switch doctors; stay with God. Your answer is not in alcohol, drugs, psychics, or even false religion. God's grace will sustain you. That same "Amazing Grace that saved a wretch like me" is also able to keep you.

The benediction found in I Peter 5:10-11 is a perfect description of the role that God's grace should have in our lives: "But the God of all grace, who hath called us unto his eternal glory by Christ Jesus, after that ye have suffered a while, make you perfect, stablish, strengthen, settle you. To him be glory and dominion for ever and ever. Amen."

Bible Study Questions

1. What vision did Paul speak about? (II Corinthians 12:1-6, KJV)
2. Where did the thorn in the flesh come from that Paul spoke about? (II Corinthians 12:7, KJV)
3. How many times did Paul go to God and ask that it be removed? (II Corinthians 12:8, KJV)
4. How did God respond to Paul's requests? (II Corinthians 12:9, KJV)
5. Do you believe that God's Grace is sufficient in your life? (Personal Reflection)

Topic: Living Water Available—No Waiting
(A man at the Pool of Bethesda waited to be healed) Scripture Reference: John 5:1-13

Insight: Instead of complaining, we need to consider Christ.

"'Sir,' the invalid replied, 'I have no one to help me into the pool when the water is stirred. While I am trying to get in, someone else goes down ahead of me'" John 5:7 (NIV).

The invalid man's excuses focused on what other people would not do for him and how other people's actions hindered him from doing for himself.

"When Jesus saw him lie, and knew that he had been now a long time in that case, he saith unto him, Wilt thou be made whole?" John 5:6 (KJV).

The man was so accustomed to elaborating on his state of helplessness that he seemed to ignore the question that Jesus asked. He immediately began telling Jesus the reason for his condition and his inability to do anything about it. Of course, Jesus knew all the circumstances and, instead of acknowledging the man's plight, issued a command of healing. "Jesus saith unto him, Rise, take up thy bed, and walk" John 5:8 (KJV).

Jesus healed the man in spite of the man's inadequate faith. In fact, he received a healing while he was trying to explain to Jesus what had prevented his healing. He may have had faith in the troubling of the water, but he had not displayed true faith in the Living Water.

The Bible states that there lay a great multitude on the five porches surrounding the Pool of Bethesda. Therefore, there was no guarantee that you would be the first to get into the water to be healed.

Jesus was speaking to the invalid man, and therefore, He had to be in close proximity to many of these people who were waiting for the troubling of the water. The "Living Water" was in their midst, but they could not see Him because they were looking out over the water instead. Today, we are looking out over troubled waters, seeking answers instead of looking to the Living Water.

It is important to note that the troubling of the water only happened during a certain season. "For an angel went down at a certain season into the pool, and troubled the water: whosoever then first after the troubling of the water stepped in was made whole of whatsoever disease he had" John 5:4 (KJV). It makes you wonder what the people were doing during the remainder of the year to secure their healing. Even today in the twenty-first century, we hear of "Miracle-Working Prophets" coming to cities to hold meetings where they will be healing the sick. We mark our calendars and anticipate the upcoming event. If we had prayed and trusted in God for a healing, if it were God's will, we would already be healed. Yet, we, like this man at the pool, are waiting to get in the crowd at the meeting. As Christians, we have to realize that what God has for us is for us.

Many times, we block our own blessings by complaining about our situation to people who can do little to solve our problems other than lending a listening ear. When we take our problems to Christ, it will become clear that He should have been our first contact.

Bible Study Questions

1. Why was there a great multitude of impotent people at the Pool of Bethesda? (John 5:4, KJV)
2. What did Jesus ask the man who had suffered with an infirmity for thirty-eight years? (John 5:6, KJV)
3. What excuses did the man offer regarding his unchanged condition? (John 5:7, KJV)
4. What instructions did Jesus give the impotent man? (John 5:8, KJV)
5. Did the man know who Jesus was? (John 5:12-13, KJV)

Topic: A Perfect Hem—No Alterations Needed
(A woman with an issue of blood sought a healing)
Scripture Reference: Mark 5:25-34; Joshua 24:15

Insight: If you are trying to get to Jesus, you have to learn to be unconcerned about consequences.

Today, it seems unimaginable that someone would suffer with a blood disease for twelve years and not receive treatment that would bring some relief. With all of the twenty-first century medical breakthroughs and research being performed on a continuous basis by brilliant minds seeking solutions to every disease imaginable, this woman's predicament cannot help but seem foreign to us.

"And a certain woman, which had an issue of blood twelve years, And had suffered many things of many physicians, and had spent all that she had, and was nothing bettered, but rather grew worse, When she had heard of Jesus, came in the press behind, and touched his garment. For she said, If I may touch but his clothes, I shall be whole" Mark 5:25-28 (KJV).

This woman's illness had driven her to despair and desperation. When hope appeared, she put her faith in gear and bulldozed her way to her healing. She had no time to consider the consequences. She had to squeeze through to seize this opportunity.

This woman had indeed suffered for twelve years with a blood disease. She had consulted numerous physicians and had spent all of her money, and there was no improvement in her condition at all. She was now desperate to find a cure.

This certain woman had reckless faith, which resulted in her bold behavior. When she heard that Jesus was in town, she made up her mind that it was now or never. She did not consider the consequence that pressing through the crowd might result in her being trampled to death. She did not consider the consequence that she might faint before she even got close enough to touch his garment. Her faith was so strong that she believed that she didn't need to make herself known to him; she only needed to touch his garment and she would be made whole.

When the woman reached Jesus and touched his clothing, she was healed of the plague. Jesus immediately felt some of his power go out of him. "And Jesus, immediately knowing in himself that virtue had gone out of him, turned him about in the press, and said, Who touched my clothes?" Mark 5:30 (KJV).

All of a sudden, there was a "Wanted" poster put up for the woman. There were no eyewitnesses and the disciples could not believe that Jesus expected them to find this woman. After all, everyone in the crowd was touching him. How were they going to find one person? Jesus could have easily picked her out of the crowd. The woman decided to turn herself in. "But the woman fearing and trembling, knowing what was done in her, came and fell down before him, and told him all the truth" Mark 5:33 (KJV).

She had to turn herself in because she knew that she did not want to trade in her healing for anything in the world. That touch was so powerful that it erased twelve years of suffering. She could not keep her silence. Jesus rewarded her for her reckless faith. "And he said unto her, Daughter, thy faith hath made thee whole; go in peace, and be whole of thy plague" Mark 5:34.

Will Jesus pick us out of a crowd today because of our faith? Or will he pick us out of a crowd because of our lack of faith? He knows our hearts and we cannot hide from Him. Let's begin operating with reckless faith. Let's develop a "whatever it takes" attitude when it comes to seeking God's presence. Don't worry about what others are doing. You have to make a decision to serve God for yourself. Remember the words of Joshua: "And if it seem evil unto you to serve the LORD, choose you this day whom ye will serve; whether the gods which your fathers served that were on the other side of the flood, or the gods of the Amorites, in whose land ye dwell: but as for me and my house, we will serve the LORD" Joshua 24:15 (KJV).

Bible Study Questions

1. What had this woman been going through for twelve years? (Mark 5:25-26, KJV)
2. How did the woman approach Jesus? (Mark 5:27-29, KJV)
3. How did Jesus respond after she touched his clothes? (Mark 5:30, KJV)
4. What was the disciples' reaction to Jesus' question about who touched him? (Mark 5:31, KJV)
5. After the woman's confession, how did Jesus pronounce her healing? (Mark 5:33-34, KJV)

Chapter 10: Don't Leave Prayer and Intercession on the Pew

Topic: A One Signature Prayer Petition

(Hezekiah petitioned God for a healing)

Scripture Reference: Isaiah 38:1-5; Hebrews 4:15-16; Romans 8:26

Insight: Jesus is our greatest prayer intercessor.

"Then Hezekiah turned his face toward the wall, and prayed unto the LORD, And said, Remember now, O LORD, I beseech thee, how I have walked before thee in truth and with a perfect heart, and have done that which is good in thy sight. And Hezekiah wept sore" Isaiah 38:2-3 (KJV).

In order to get the answer that he needed, Hezekiah had to go to the "Answer." It is a blessing to have other people pray for you, but there are some things that you have to take to God for yourself. Hezekiah didn't even ask Isaiah to pray to God for him. Hezekiah realized that he had to present his own petition to God.

Many times in court cases, the defense attorney advises the defendant not to take the stand. This sometimes proves to be a winning strategy; however, in many cases, it has the adverse effect. There are some prayer petitions that we must present to God on our own behalf. When you are facing trials where you need the kind of peace "that passeth all understanding," I strongly suggest that you take the stand.

As Christians, when we petition God, there is also a process that we have to follow to ensure that our petitions get into the right hands. In Hebrews 4:16, it states: "Let us therefore come boldly unto the throne of grace, that we may obtain mercy, and find grace to help in time of need." When we get to the throne of grace, we have to pray in the name of Jesus. Once we start to pray in Jesus' name, the Holy Ghost takes a look at the petition and goes into action. Romans 8:26 says: "Likewise the Spirit also helpeth our infirmities: for we know not what we should pray for as we ought: but the Spirit itself maketh intercession for us with groanings which cannot be uttered."

The petition is then placed in the hands of Jesus. Jesus lived on earth as a man and experienced both the joys and sorrows that we experience, and He already knows what we are going through. "For we have not an high priest that cannot be touched with the feelings of our infirmities: but was in all points tempted like as we are, yet without sin" Hebrews 4:15 (KJV).

When Jesus gets ready to put his signature on our petition, He doesn't ask Gabriel to sharpen a number 2 pencil. He doesn't say to Michael the archangel, "Go and find me a Bic pen so I can sign this petition." Jesus signs his signature in the blood that he shed on Calvary for our sins.

Once the petition gets to God, God only sees one signature. Your signature is covered up by the blood from Jesus' signature. There's no need for God to verify any signatures because he recognizes the blood. So whatever blessings you are asking for according to God's will, even if Satan tries to list your sins next to your signature, God is willing to forgive them because he recognizes the blood. Thank God for the blood of Jesus!

Bible Study Questions

1. What declaration did Isaiah bring to Hezekiah from God? (Isaiah 38:1, KJV)
2. How did Hezekiah react to the news that Isaiah brought? (Isaiah 38:2, KJV)
3. What was Hezekiah's petition to God? (Isaiah 38:3, KJV)
4. How did God respond to Hezekiah's prayers? (Isaiah 38:4-5, KJV)
5. Do you know how to go to God in prayer on your own behalf? (Personal Reflection)

Topic: God Attends Midnight Prayer Services

(Paul and Silas held a prayer service)

Scripture Reference: Acts 16:22-31; Psalm 61:2

Insight: Praising God is an important element in effective prayers.

"And at midnight Paul and Silas prayed, and sang praises unto God: and the prisoners heard them" Acts 16:25.

When we get into trouble, our praise is received by God as a pleasing prelude to our petitions. Wouldn't it be wonderful to know what prayer was prayed and what song was sung to cause God to respond the way that He did? The prayer and song belonged to Paul and Silas, and that was the right prayer and song for them to offer to God at the right time, which was midnight.

We should have our own song and prayer for the midnights in our lives. Maybe they sang "Father I Stretch My Hands to Thee" and maybe they prayed like David, "From the end of the earth will I cry unto thee, when my heart is overwhelmed: lead me to the rock that is higher than I" Psalm 61:2 (KJV). They were certainly in overwhelming circumstances. Having been beaten and thrown into prison with no relief in sight, they chose not to complain but to hold a prayer service. Whatever prayer was prayed and whatever song was sung, it reached God and his response was one that was literally earth shaking. "And suddenly there was a great earthquake, so that the foundations of the prison were shaken: and immediately all the doors were opened, and everyone's bands were loosed" Acts 16:26 (KJV).

After the earthquake had taken place and all the prison doors were open, the keeper of the prison just knew that all the prisoners had fled. He then made a quick decision to pull his sword and kill himself.

No doubt the keeper of the prison knew that he would be facing death once the news of this prison escape reached the magistrates.

Before he could do himself harm, the Bible tells us that Paul cried out with a loud voice to let him know that no one had escaped. Not only did Paul save the jailer's life, he would later lead him to Christ so that his soul could be saved. "Then he called for a light, and sprang in, and came trembling, and fell down before Paul and Silas, And brought them out, and said, Sirs, what must I do to be saved? And they said, Believe on the Lord Jesus Christ, and thou shalt be saved, and thy house" Acts 16:29-31.

God listens to all sincere prayers. It seems as though He is especially attentive to prayers that go up at midnight. When you pray at midnight, you are sending up a prayer about all of your cares on this side of midnight and you are praying for strength to face the challenges of the new day that is on the other side of midnight. God never sleeps, so He loves to hear from you at midnight. The same way we celebrate the coming of a new year with fanfare, we should celebrate every new day that we are blessed to see.

The jailer discovered that the security in the prison could not be compared to the safety and security that God provides.

Bible Study Questions

1. How did Paul and Silas react to being thrown into prison? (Acts 16:25, KJV)
2. What was God's response to Paul and Silas's prayers? (Acts 16:26, KJV)
3. What question did the jailer ask about Salvation? (Acts 16:30, KJV)
4. Why didn't the prisoners escape once the prison doors were opened? (Personal Reflection)
5. Have you ever had to call on God at midnight? Were you able to feel His presence as He listened to your prayers? (Personal Reflection)

Topic: Facing a Fruitless Future
(A dresser of the vineyard interceded for a fig tree)
Scripture Reference: Luke 13: 6-9; Matthew 13:24-30; Matthew 25:13

Insight: The sin in our lives hinders our fruit-producing process.

"Then said he unto the dresser of his vineyard, Behold, these three years I come seeking fruit on this fig tree, and find none: cut it down; why cumbereth it the ground?" Luke 13:7 (KJV).

When God reserves the just punishment that we deserve, we call it another chance, but it is really another measure of His mercy.

Thank God that He is not a "God of Zero Tolerance." Many people call God a "God of a Second Chance." However, a better description is that he is a "God of Abundant Mercies."

The owner of the vineyard expected a return on his investment in this fig tree. As the owner of the vineyard, he was entitled to do whatever he chose to do with the trees in the vineyard. The parable does not indicate the reason why the owner of the vineyard chose this specific year to render his decision about the fig tree. Perhaps on the first year, the owner might have decided not to act hastily and allowed the tree another year to produce fruit. The second year that he came looking for fruit, he might have taken into consideration that there had been some weather conditions or insects that posed a problem. However, on the third year that the owner came looking for fruit, he realized that a decision had to be made.

"'Sir,' the man replied, 'leave it alone for one more year, and I'll dig around it and fertilize it. If it bears fruit next year, fine! If not, then cut it down.'" Luke 13:8-9 (NIV).

The dresser was forced to plead for mercy on behalf of the fig tree. He was forced to take a step of faith. He needed to convince the owner that he could turn the situation around for the fig tree in order to preserve it and not have the owner cut it down.

The owner of the vineyard had exhausted his patience with the fig tree. When he returned to the vineyard and saw no fruit, he decided that the time for patience was over.

The dresser of the vineyard became the intercessor for the fig tree. He asked the owner of the vineyard for another year so that he could give the fig tree some extra attention. He wanted to give the tree more fertilizer and water. He would take special attention to the pruning of the tree. He realized that the survival of the fig tree was in his hands. He was willing to make whatever sacrifices he needed to make to ensure that the tree lived. Sound familiar? We were once like this fig tree. We were about to be cut off by the owner of the vineyard until Jesus became the dresser of the vineyard and went to the cross on our behalf.

Today, gardeners use a product called "Miracle Grow." But long before this product was invented, the blood that Jesus shed on Calvary ran down and penetrated the sin-sick soil of our souls. Now that was truly "Miracle Grow."

Many of us have had many more years than this fig tree to produce fruit, yet we have nothing to show for our years of professing Christianity. In Matthew 13:24-30 (KJV), Jesus used the parable of the sower to warn us of the dangers of being unproductive Christians.

Jesus sits at the right hand of God, making intercession for us. Can you imagine the plea that Jesus makes for us: "Father, I know they are not living according to your will; but Father please give them another measure of mercy." Just as the dresser of the vineyard did not know the exact time when the owner of the vineyard would return, we do not know when Jesus will return to inspect our fruit. "Watch therefore, for ye know neither the day nor the hour wherein the Son of man cometh" Matthew 25:13 (KJV).

Bible Study Questions

1. What tree was inspected by the owner of the vineyard? (Luke 13:1, KJV)
2. After the third year, what did the owner instruct the dresser of the vineyard to do? (Luke 13:7, KJV)
3. What was the dresser of the vineyard's reaction to the owner's instruction? (Luke 13:8, KJV)
4. What alternative did the dresser of the vineyard offer the owner? (Luke 13:9, KJV)
5. If we, as Christians, are not bearing good fruit, what will happen to us? (Matthew 7:18-20, KJV)

Topic: A Father's Gracious Prayer for His Son
(David prayed to God for Solomon's success)
Scripture Reference: I Chronicles 28:1-10; Chapter 29 KJV

Insight: A sincere prayer begins with love.

As parents, we only want the best for our children. We have to learn to go to God in prayer and pour out our hearts on behalf of our children.

Many times, as human beings, we find it difficult to pray unselfish prayers. However, when it comes to praying for our children, selfishness should never enter into our thoughts. When you feel the need to pray a sincere, gracious prayer for your child, you can find inspiration by reading the prayer that David prayed to God for his son, Solomon. David's prayer was a great example of his "generosity of spirit," which endeared him to God.

David was told by God that he would not be the king who would build a house for God, but that it would be his son, Solomon. David was not upset that Solomon had been chosen to build God's house. Some selfish parents are envious of their own children. David was more concerned about Solomon's success and he wanted to ensure that Solomon knew what was required when it came to serving God.

David then gave instructions to Solomon. "And thou, Solomon my son, know thou the God of thy father, and serve him with a perfect heart and with a willing mind: for the LORD searcheth all hearts, and understandeth all the imaginations of the thoughts: if thou seek him, he will be found of thee; but if thou forsake him, he will cast thee off for ever. Take heed now; for the LORD hath chosen thee to build an house for the sanctuary: be strong, and do it" I Chronicles 28:9-10 (KJV).

David then instructed the people that they were to accept Solomon as God's choice to build the temple. However, they were also to do their part. "Furthermore David the king said unto all the congregation, Solomon my son, whom alone God hath chosen, is yet young and tender, and the work is great: for the palace is not for man, but for the Lord God" I Chronicles 29:1. David wanted the congregation to know that Solomon had his support and also needed their cooperation.

David realized that all of the sacrifices he had made, as well as the sacrifices he admonished the people to make in order to build the temple, were not really sacrifices. They were simply returning a portion of the blessings God had so generously given to them.

Many times, when it comes to our young-adult children, we take the "I'll just sit back and let them learn the hard way" attitude. We feel that they will not listen to us anyway and that we are wasting our breath. If we had the kind of love that David had for God and for Solomon, we would not consider it a waste of our breath to try and get through to our children. First of all, if you love God, you are not going to tell your child anything that is not true and you will certainly not allow them to fail without trying to give them some direction.

When we reach the point with our children and throw up our hands and voice the words, "I'm just going to put you in the hands of the Lord," please consider that there is a right and a wrong way to proceed with that action. Instead of just saying, "Lord, I'm through. I'm putting them in your hands," think about the prayer that David prayed for Solomon.

We all want our children to have bright futures, and David was no different. He knew that the one thing he could do to ensure

Solomon's success was to pray and ask God to guide Solomon's steps. "And give unto Solomon my son a perfect heart, to keep thy commandments, thy testimonies, and thy statutes, and to do all these things, and to build the palace, for the which I have made provision" I Chronicles 29:19 (KJV).

Our sons and daughters may not be facing such a daunting task as building a house for God, but whatever they are facing, David's prayer can certainly be incorporated into our own. David's prayer to God resulted in great success for his son, Solomon. "Then Solomon sat on the throne of the LORD as king instead of David his father, and prospered; and all Israel obeyed him. And all the princes, and the mighty men, and all the sons likewise of king David, submitted themselves unto Solomon the king. And the LORD magnified Solomon exceedingly in the sight of all Israel, and bestowed upon him such royal majesty as had not been on any king before him in Israel" I Chronicles 29:23-25 (KJV).

Bible Study Questions

1. Why did God appoint Solomon to build the temple instead of allowing David to carry out the task? (I Chronicles 28:2-6 KJV)
2. What did David do to help ensure Solomon's success? (I Chronicles 29:19 KJV)

3. Have you ever really prayed an unselfish prayer and not asked for anything for yourself? (Personal Reflection)
4. Have you ever had to cry out to God on behalf of your child? (Personal Reflection)
5. Have you witnessed God's blessings in your child's life as a result of your prayer? (Personal Reflection)

Chapter 11: Don't Leave Faith on the Pew

Topic: A Determined Mind Becomes Distracted

(Peter walked on the water to meet Jesus)

Scripture Reference: Matthew14:22-33

Insight: We have to learn to concentrate on Christ and not on our conditions.

"And straightway Jesus constrained his disciples to get into a ship, and to go before him unto the other side, while he sent the multitudes away" Matthew 14:22 (KJV).

While Jesus prayed alone on the shore, the disciples were in the ship in the midst of the sea, with the ship being tossed by the waves. Jesus began to walk on the sea toward the ship, and the disciples saw him and became afraid, thinking that he was a ghost. Jesus spoke to them so that they would calm down. "But straightway Jesus spake unto them, saying, Be of good cheer; it is I; be not afraid" Matthew 14:27 (KJV).

Once Peter, who seemed to be the risk-taker of the twelve, heard Jesus' voice, he wanted to verify if it really were Jesus. "And

Peter answered him and said, Lord, if it be thou, bid me come unto thee on the water" Matthew 14:28 (KJV). Jesus did not try to explain to Peter that it was really him. He simply said, "Come." Once Peter got out of the ship and began to walk toward Jesus, it seemed as though he was going to reach Jesus, but then he took his eyes off Jesus and began to focus on the wind. "But when he saw the wind boisterous, he was afraid; and beginning to sink, he cried, saying, Lord, save me" Matthew 14:30.

Of course, Jesus saved him, but Jesus also questioned Peter's lack of faith. "And immediately Jesus stretched forth his hand, and caught him, and said unto him, O thou of little faith, wherefore didst thou doubt?" Matthew 14:31 (KJV). What a wonderful example of the love that Jesus has for us. It is important to note that the Scripture says Jesus "caught him" (Peter) before he asked him the question "wherefore didst thou doubt?" As loving parents, we sometimes yell at our children in the midst of solving their problems, and then continue to rant and rave after we get them out of the situation. Many times, we bring the issue up again when we get angry.

Jesus didn't question Peter until he secured his safety. Jesus is so forgiving that he didn't hold Peter's lack of faith against him. The Scripture does not say that when Peter later denied Jesus that Jesus said, "I knew you would deny me. Remember when I had to save you from drowning because you looked down and took your eyes off me?"

Unlike us, Jesus' love is not based on conditions. Thank God he has unconditional love for us.

A baby's first nourishment comes in the form of milk. The baby's diet later changes to cereal and baby food, and then switches to a diet of solid food and meat. When we read the story of the disciples being fearful of the storm and afraid as they saw Jesus walking on the water, it appears that at this stage in the lives of the disciples, they were not ready to switch to a diet of solid food and meat. As many miracles as the disciples had already witnessed, you would think that they would not doubt the power of Jesus. Their focus had switched from Christ to their circumstances.

We cannot be too critical of the disciples for forgetting the miracles because today, we sometimes become too focused on the miracles. Today, many of us are trying to survive on a vitamin "B Blessed" Diet: bless me and bless me so I will continue to believe. What will happen when the blessings stop and we go from good health to poor health, from a great job to no job, from Mo Money to no money, and from happy family reunions to family funerals? Let us become mature Christians and learn to survive on a Diet of Faith.

We cannot be too critical of Peter, either. How many of us would have stepped out onto the water without hesitation? The story teaches us that faith without focus fails. We have to keep our focus on Jesus no matter how dark the situation appears. "Now faith is the substance of things hoped for, the evidence of things not seen" Hebrews

11:1 (KJV). Has God ever worked a miracle in your life? Do you still question his power? Believe that if God did it then, He can do it now.

Bible Study Questions

1. What was Jesus doing after he sent the multitudes away and instructed the disciples to get in a ship and cross over to the other side? (Matthew 14:22-23, KJV)
2. When the disciples' ship reached the middle of the sea, how was the ship affected by the waves and the wind? (Matthew 14:24, KJV)
3. How did the disciples react to seeing Jesus walking on the water? (Matthew 14:25-26, KJV)
4. What did Jesus say to calm the disciples? (Matthew 14:27, KJV)
5. What happened when Peter tried to reach Jesus by walking on the water? (Matthew 14:28-31, KJV)

Topic: A Relocation Package for Ruth
(Ruth had the courage to follow Naomi)
Scripture Reference: The book of Ruth

Insight: As followers of Christ, your lifestyle will always be scrutinized by the world.

"And Ruth said, Entreat me not to leave thee, or to return from following after thee: for whither thou goest, I will go; and where thou lodgest, I will lodge: thy people shall be my people, and thy God my God" Ruth 1:16a (KJV).

In some job markets, there are companies that offer lucrative relocation packages in order to secure some of the top professionals in their field. Many of these recruits come from outside the state and require relocation. The top job candidates are offered relocation packages that include homes, lucrative pay, and incentives that make it difficult to turn down positions.

In Ruth's situation, not only was Naomi not able to offer her a relocation package, she essentially tried talking her out of relocating. Ruth, however, begged Naomi to allow her to accompany her on the journey to Naomi's homeland. The average person would probably have looked at Naomi's life and said, "Now that's a lady who is plagued by bad luck. No way I'm following her." However, Ruth had witnessed the faith that her mother-in-law had in her God no matter what situation she faced in life. Naomi had lost a husband and two sons, and was now embarking on a trip to her homeland.

Ruth chose to follow Naomi and Naomi's God. "Where thou diest, will I die, and there will I be buried: the LORD do so to me, and more also, if ought but death part thee and me" Ruth 1:17. Ruth had no idea where they would stay or how they would survive when they arrived in Bethlehem. She must have had some faith that Naomi's God would take care of them. When Ruth found her way to Boaz's field, she also found her way into his heart. Naomi was familiar with the customs and advised Ruth on how she should conduct herself to let Boaz know that she was interested in him.

I remember growing up and watching my mother mix cake batter. She did not own an electric mixer, so all the mixing was done by hand. My brother and I would stand and watch as she beat the cake mixture, which seemed to take forever. We never left our post because we knew what was in store for us once she finished. My mother knew that allowing us to lick the bowl after she had filled the cake pans was our special treat. She always left extra batter on the sides of the bowl. She could have scraped much more of the batter into the cake pans, but she always left us a little extra in the bowl.

My brother and I would take our fingers and go round and round the bowl, wiping it as clean as we could. My brother was content with the mix from the sides of the bowl and also content with leaving me to clean the kitchen. I didn't mind because my extra effort meant I ended up with the mixing spoon, which contained a large serving of the cake batter.

Boaz ensured that more than a little extra was left for Ruth. "And when she was risen up to glean, Boaz commanded his young men, saying, Let her glean even among the sheaves, and reproach her not: And left all also some of the handfuls of purpose for her, and leave them, that she may glean them, and rebuke her not" Ruth 2:15-

16 (KJV). Because of Ruth's loyalty to her mother-in-law and her unselfishness in working to provide for her mother-in-law's needs, Boaz recognized honorable qualities in Ruth.

Boaz accepted the role of kinsman redeemer and he and Ruth were married. When their son, Obed, was born Naomi was also blessed. "And he shall be unto thee a restorer of thy life, and a nourisher of thine old age: for thy daughter in law, which loveth thee, which is better to thee than seven sons, hath born him" Ruth 4:15. The ultimate reward in Ruth's relocation package was that she learned to trust in the awesome power of God.

Bible Study Questions

1. What commitment did Ruth make to Naomi? (Ruth 1:16-17, KJV)
2. Why did Naomi return to Bethlehem? (Ruth 1:6, KJV)
3. What did Ruth do to provide for Naomi? (Ruth 2:2, KJV)
4. Whose field did Ruth work in? (Ruth 2:3, KJV)
5. How was Ruth blessed in Naomi's homeland? (Ruth 4:13, KJV)

Topic: Life without a Lifeboat

(Paul survived a shipwreck)

Scripture Reference: Acts, Chapter 27; Matthew 28:19-20

Insight: You are in good company if you spend your time with people who have a personal relationship with God.

Paul had been imprisoned for two years and was appealing his case to a court in Rome, which, at that time, was no doubt the equivalent to our Supreme Court in the United States. Paul was being transported by ship along with certain other prisoners. A centurion by the name of Julius was put in charge of the prisoners. Julius treated Paul well and even allowed him to go ashore at Sidon to visit his friends and refresh himself. When they reached Myra, a city of Lycia, the centurion transferred Paul and the other prisoners to a ship that was sailing to Italy.

The ship was sailing slowly and not covering very much territory because the wind was not cooperating on this voyage. As the captain of the ship made the decision to sail from fair havens, Paul tried to warn them that this was not a good idea. The centurion decided to dismiss Paul's advice and listened to the captain. They sailed to Phenice, where they later encountered a tempestuous wind called Euroclydon, which was a terrible east wind. Eventually, they had to allow the ship to be carried by the wind.

Paul encouraged them by telling them that the angel of God had appeared to him and told him know that none of them would die. Paul let them know that the ship would be destroyed but they would be saved. As they continued to encounter dangerous seas, the shipmen were about to flee the ship, yet Paul told them that they would have to remain on the ship or they could not be saved. "Paul said to the centurion and to the soldiers, Except these abide in the ship, ye cannot be saved" Acts 27:31 (KJV).

Eventually, the ship ran aground and began to break apart. The soldiers decided to kill the prisoners, fearing that they would swim out and escape. But God had his arms of protection around Paul. "But the centurion, willing to save Paul, kept them from their purpose; and commanded that they which could swim should cast themselves first into the sea, and get to land: And the rest, some on boards, and some on broken pieces of the ship. And so it came to pass, that they escaped all safe to land" Acts 27:43-44 (KJV).

Imagine putting your faith in a piece of board for your survival. At that moment, the men who could not swim had to rely on planks of the ship because they did not know how to swim. Faith in the planks became a necessity.

They were probably thinking at that moment, *If I survive, I will learn to swim before I get on another ship*. They had forgotten the dream Paul told them about. In Paul's dream, the ship would be wrecked, but everyone would survive.

The ones who could swim jumped in first and made it to land. They were then able to help the ones coming in on planks and broken pieces of the ship. No doubt some made it almost to the shore, but being so frightful at the prospect of being in so much water and clinging only to a plank, they must have imagined that the distance to land was farther than it actually was.

In life, we often sail on ships that sometimes run aground. If we are trusting in the true and living God, we realize that even if the ship breaks apart, he has already equipped us so that we can reach land safely.

Paul was the blessed passenger on the ship, and because of God's favor on Paul, everyone was saved. We need to be around people who have God's favor and pattern our actions after them. You will find them not only carrying a Bible, but studying and living by it. You will find them following the commandments and not just talking about them. Most of all, you will see them display love.

Once you develop a personal relationship with God, you will be able to reach out to those who are sinking in the sea of sin and give them encouragement. We are commissioned to spread the good news. "Go ye therefore, and teach all nations, baptizing them in the name of the Father, and of the Son, and of the Holy Ghost: Teaching them to observe all things whatsoever I have commanded you: and lo, I am with you always, even unto the end of the world" Matthew 28:19-20.

Bible Study Questions

1. What did the Angel of God say to Paul about this voyage? (Acts 27:18-24, KJV)

2. What did Paul tell the centurion and the soldiers about remaining on the ship? (Acts 27:31, KJV)
3. What happened when the ship ran aground? (Acts 27:40-41, KJV)
4. What did the soldiers decide to do to keep the prisoners from escaping? (Acts 27:42, KJV)
5. How were the prisoners who could not swim able to reach land? (Acts 27:43-44, KJV)

Topic: Something to Shout About
(Joshua followed God's marching orders)
Scripture Reference: Joshua 6:1-20

Insight: We have to go through certain experiences to discover God's purpose for our lives.

God gave Joshua specific instructions regarding the capture of Jericho. Joshua was not instructed to launch a great battle or given plans of attack. Instead, he received marching orders. "And ye shall compass the city, all ye men of war, and go round about the city once. Thus shalt thou do six days" Joshua 6:3 (KJV).

The armed men were to be at the head of the procession. Seven priests were to go before the Ark of the Covenant with trumpets of rams' horns and the other men followed the ark. They were to march around the city once a day for six days, and on the seventh day, they were to march around the city seven times.

During the six days of marching, the people were to remain silent; the only sounds were to come from the trumpets that the priests were blowing. "And it came to pass, when Joshua had spoken unto the people, that the seven priests bearing the seven trumpets of rams' horns passed on before the LORD, and blew with the trumpets: and the ark of the covenant of the LORD followed them" Joshua 6:8 (KJV).

On the seventh day, after the people had marched around the city seven times, when the priests sounded the trumpets, then and only then were they to shout. They were told that God would give them the city following their shout. "And it came to pass at the seventh time, when the priests blew with the trumpets, Joshua said unto the people Shout; for the Lord hath given you the city" Joshua 6:16 (KJV).

God could have given the city of Jericho to his chosen people at any time. However, there was a reason why the people had been instructed to march for seven days.

The first day of marching represented unity—one march, one accord.

The second day of marching represented fellowship. God was teaching them to not only work together but to be concerned about each other.

The third day of marching was the first step in perseverance. March number three showed that they were committed to staying the course and being obedient to God. In the same way that Jesus was an obedient participant in the Trinity as the Son of God, the Israelites, too, had to be obedient.

The fourth day of marching was also a significant day. The number four represented the earth and its four corners. The earth was made solid in creation. By the time the marchers made the fourth trek around the city, they became solidified. God was showing them that he was able to keep them together with no break in the ranks and no deserters.

The fifth day of marching represented God's grace. No matter what had transpired in the past, God was still showing them grace because they were still not worthy of the blessings that they were receiving.

The sixth day of marching represented man's human weakness. God provided them with the strength that they needed after marching around the city for five days. They were able to draw courage from the knowledge that God was with them and that the victory would surely come just as God had promised.

The seventh day of marching represented the completion and evidence of God's power. Once they shouted, the wall surrounding the city fell. "So the people shouted when the priests blew with the trumpets: and it came to pass, when the people heard the sound of the trumpet, and the people shouted with a great shout, that the wall fell down flat, so that the people went up into the city, every man straight before him, and they took the city" Joshua 6:20 (KJV).

Not only had Joshua shown uncompromising faith in God, but that same faith had been instilled in the marchers. They had learned about patience, perseverance, and the power of God.

The people of Jericho had confidence that the wall was their stronghold. However, they discovered that the wall could not withstand God's purpose and plan. The Israelites followed God's plan and prevailed. As Christians, we face situations in our lives that seem reinforced by walls that cannot be penetrated. If we put our trust in God, we will learn that all things are possible with God.

You are probably thinking, *Well, I could follow God's plan for seven days if I knew that the victory was assured on the seventh day.* That seven-day victory was for the Israelites. Your victory may take seven weeks or seven months or seven years, or it could take seven minutes.

We have to realize that God has already planned and purposed our victories. The lesson to be learned from the Jericho story is that God wants us to be silent and listen for his voice, and not be deceived by another. We must pray without ceasing; be patient and be ready to shout when the victory comes.

Bible Study Questions

1. What were the marching orders given to Joshua for the first six days? (Joshua 6:1-3, KJV)

2. How was the seventh day of marching different? (Joshua 6:15-16, KJV)
3. What do you think the people of Jericho thought of this daily parade of marchers? (Personal Reflection)
4. Have you learned to be silent and listen to God's voice? (Personal Reflection)
5. Do you really know when to shout? (Personal Reflection)

Chapter 12: Don't Leave Humility on the Pew

Topic: Taking a Faith Inventory—Time to Reorder

(A father admitted that he had some unbelief)

Scripture Reference: Mark 9:19-23

Insight: God already knows the degree of our faith.

"He answereth him, and saith, O faithless generation how long shall I be with you? How long shall I suffer you? Bring him unto me" Mark 9:19 (KJV).

A request for help from Jesus usually comes when someone is in a desperate situation. There was a boy possessed with a demon whose father came to Jesus to request that his son be healed. The father initially asked the disciples to heal his son, but they could not.

Before He would heal the boy, Jesus let the father of the boy know that his faith would be included as a part of this healing process. "Jesus said unto him, If thou canst believe, all things are possible to him that believeth" Mark 9:23.

The father faced the proposition that his lack of faith might in some way hinder his son's healing. He realized that it was necessary that he told Jesus the truth about the extent of his faith. "And straightway the father of the child cried out, and said with tears, Lord, I believe, help thou mine unbelief" Mark 9:24. This father immediately let Jesus know that his faith was inadequate. The father was not only begging for his son's life, but was asking Jesus for a healing for his (the father's) own sin sick soul.

The father had enough faith to bring his son to Jesus. The question is: did he have enough faith to believe that Jesus could really heal him? Once the father realized that his faith was not at the level that it should be, he immediately confessed to Jesus that there was some faith there, but not enough.

Many times, we take our problems to Jesus, yet almost before we can turn to walk away, we begin to wonder whether he will really solve them. We begin to try and take on the role that only Jesus can fill, and that is the role of Problem Solver. Here is where our own unbelief begins to manifest itself. We may need to pray as this father did. We may need to say, "Lord, I have enough faith to bring you the problems, but help my unbelief and remove all doubts as to your power to solve them."

As stated earlier, the father first brought his son to the disciples to be healed. How many people have we talked to about our problems before we brought them to the Master? How many psychic hotlines have we called? How many so-called friends have we put our trust in? How many false religions have we turned to? Only to discover that like this boy, the demons remained. Or maybe we took our problems to sincere people of God and they tried to solve them, but as Jesus said, maybe the problems could only be solved by prayer and fasting. Start with Jesus who is, was, and will always be the Answer.

Bible Study Questions

1. When the father of the demonic boy asked that his son be healed, what was Jesus' reply? (Mark 9:21-23, KJV)
2. How did the father respond to Jesus' statement regarding faith? (Mark 9:24, KJV)
3. What command did Jesus give to the foul spirit? (Mark 9:25, KJV)
4. Why couldn't the disciples heal the boy? (Mark 9:28-29, KJV)
5. Are we willing to admit that we believe, yet there is some unbelief? (Personal Reflection)

Topic: Recognizing the Power of Jesus
(Jesus showed mercy because of the faith of a centurion)
Scripture Reference: Matthew 8:5-13

Insight: Many times, individuals outside the "religious circles" are better able to recognize God's authority.

"The centurion answered and said, Lord, I am not worthy that thou shouldest come under my roof: but speak the word only, and my servant shall be healed" Matthew 8:8 (KJV).

During a time when most of Jesus' followers who professed to be believers, yet were still looking for signs to reinforce their belief, a story of an unbeliever who displayed more belief than Jesus' own followers unfolded. Jesus was entering into Capernaum and was approached by a centurion: "And when Jesus was entered into Capernaum, there came unto him a centurion, beseeching him, And saying, Lord, my servant lieth at home sick of the palsy, grievously tormented" Matthew 8:5-6 (KJV).

First of all, note that the centurion was not petitioning Jesus to heal a member of his family, not his son or daughter, but he was requesting that his servant be healed. He could probably have replaced this ill servant with a healthy one without difficulty. The fact that he asked for this servant to be healed revealed the compassion of the centurion.

When Jesus agreed to go to his home to heal his servant, the centurion's knowledge of Jesus' holiness began to surface. He let Jesus know that he (the centurion) was not worthy for Jesus to come under his roof. "The centurion answered and said, Lord, I am not worthy that thou shouldest come under my roof: but speak the word only, and my servant shall be healed" Matthew 8:8 (KJV).

Surely, the centurion was not ashamed of his home because he must have been a man of some means to own servants. He was wise enough to realize that he was unclean. "But we are all as an unclean thing, and all our righteousnesses are as filthy rags; and we all do fade as a leaf; and our iniquities, like the wind, have taken us away" Isaiah 64:6 (KJV).

As Christians today, it is not easy for us to acknowledge our unworthiness. Many of us feel that we are living lives that we would have no problem saying, "Sure, Jesus, come on over. Just give me a few hours to tidy up the place." We might even ask Jesus to delay his visit for a day or two, so that we could call a maid service to make sure that there was not a speck of dust around.

We fail to realize that Jesus will not be coming back to inspect our houses to see if there are stains on our carpets. He's coming back to see if we are holding up the bloodstained banner. He's coming after those who are covered under his blood.

Many of us have egos that keep us from recognizing that we are filthy rags in God's sight. We believe that our personal accomplishments should be a testimony to our characters. Personal achievements may enhance one's notoriety, but they do not create character. Belief in Christ, confession of our sins and inadequacies, surrendering of our will to God's will, and the application of biblical principles in our lives are what truly create character.

The centurion acknowledged Jesus' power: "but speak the word only and my servant shall be healed" Matthew 8:8b (KJV). The centurion went on to let Jesus know why he believed that it was not necessary for Jesus to be in the same room with his servant for the healing to take place. "For I am a man under authority, having soldiers under me: and I say to this man, Go, and he goeth; and to another, Come, and he cometh; and to my servant, Do this, and he doeth it" Matthew 8:9 (KJV).

The centurion recognized the power of one in authority and he recognized the degree of the authority that Jesus had. He had acknowledged that Jesus was Master over sickness and death, and was the commander of cures. He simply needed to say to the cure for palsy, go to the home of the centurion, and cure his servant. The Scripture tells of Jesus' reaction to the centurion's faith. "When Jesus heard it, he marvelled, and said to them that followed, Verily I say unto you, I have not found so great faith, no, not in Israel" Matthew 8:10 (KJV).

As always, Jesus rewards true faith: "And Jesus said unto the centurion, Go thy way; and as thou hast believed, so be it done unto thee. And his servant was healed in the selfsame hour" Matthew 8:13.

Jesus wanted his followers to know that even those who confessed to be believers had not exemplified the faith of this centurion. The fact that he recognized the power of Jesus' words and the scope of Jesus' authority was something that caused Jesus to point out his faith.

Jesus went on to let his followers know that there would be some in the kingdom who felt that they belonged there. However, as soon as they got comfortable and staked out their cloud, they would be sent in another direction. "And I say unto you, That many shall come from the east and west, and shall sit down with Abraham, and Isaac, and Jacob, in the kingdom of heaven. But the children of the kingdom shall be cast out into outer darkness: there shall be weeping and gnashing of teeth" Matthew 8:11-12.

How many of us really know just how powerful we are because of our relationship with Jesus? There is a reason that we pray in the name of Jesus. That is the name that God recognizes above all other names. Jesus can speak a word and change any situation around in the blink of an eye.

Bible Study Questions

1. How did the centurion respond when Jesus offered to go to his house? (Matthew 8:8, KJV)
2. How did the centurion expect Jesus to heal his servant? (Matthew 8:8-9, KJV)
3. What did the centurion say that illustrated he recognized Jesus' authority? (Matthew 8:9, KJV)
4. What did Jesus say about the centurion's faith? (Matthew 8:10-13, KJV)
5. Do we really recognize how much power is in the name of Jesus? (Personal Reflection)

Topic: Looking for the Red Carpet
(Naaman expected the royal treatment)
Scripture Reference: II Kings 5:1-15

Insight: Authentic character is found when we learn to pull back man's artificial layers.

"And she said unto her mistress, Would God my lord were with the prophet that is in Samaria! for he would recover him of his leprosy" II Kings 5:3 (KJV).

Naaman was a high-ranking Syrian officer. You could say that he had the king of Syria's ear. One would imagine that Naaman was living the life. However, there was one thing that prevented Naaman from relaxing in his Jacuzzi. With all his honors, Naaman could not escape the fact that he was a leper.

Outward appearances sometimes cause us to be reluctant when it comes to taking the advice of others. We have to realize that God does not always send us answers packaged the way we anticipate. Many times, the gift wrapped in plain brown paper is more valuable than the gift in the shiny, wrapped, and bow-adorned box.

Visiting dignitaries from foreign countries receive the red carpet treatment when they arrive at the White House in Washington, D.C. People of high rank and importance have come to expect the red carpet treatment. When attending award shows, celebrities look forward to walking on the red carpet and being seen by their peers and adoring fans. Many of these stars spend thousands of dollars on designer outfits so that they can gain the coveted recognition of being the best-dressed person to walk on the red carpet. British designer Debbie Wingham is credited with designing the most expensive dress in the world. A model slinked onto the catwalk in September of 2012 wearing the dress that Wingham designed, a black diamond dress priced at $5.7 million dollars. I wonder what army was guarding her?

When the king of Israel received the dispatch from the king of Syria that he was sending Naaman to Israel to be healed, he became distraught. When Elisha heard that the king was in despair, he sent a message to the king to calm his fears. "And it was so, when Elisha the man of God had heard that the king of Israel had rent his clothes, that he sent to the king, saying, Wherefore hast thou rent thy clothes? let him come now to me, and he shall know that there is a prophet in Israel" II Kings 5:8.

When Naaman arrived at the door of Elisha's house, there was no red carpet rolled out for him to enter the house. In fact, he was not allowed inside the door of Elisha's house. Elisha sent a messenger out with instructions for Naaman. "And Elisha sent a messenger unto him, saying, Go and wash in Jordan seven times, and thy flesh shall come again to thee, and thou shalt be clean" II Kings 5:10 (KJV).

That sounded simple enough. However, both the simplicity of the prescribed treatment and the lack of recognition for his position as captain of the Syrian army were considered by Naaman to be totally unacceptable. "But Naaman went away angry and said, 'I thought that he would surely come out to me and stand and call on the name of the LORD his God, wave his hand over the spot and cure me of my leprosy'" II Kings 5:11 (NIV). Naaman was so upset that he refused to follow the instructions. He decided that if washing in a river was all that was required to heal him, then he could do that in his own land, where the rivers were much cleaner than the Jordan.

Once again, God would choose to use people who seemed unlikely choices to men to bring resolutions to seemingly insurmountable issues. "And his servants came near, and spake unto him, and said, My father, if the prophet had bid thee do some great thing, wouldest thou not have done it? how much rather then, when he saith to thee, Wash, and be clean?" II Kings 5:13. The servants of Naaman convinced him to follow Elisha's instructions.

Naaman went and washed in the Jordan seven times, and he was cured of his leprosy. Naaman acknowledged the God of Israel as the true God. All of a sudden, the red carpet treatment was insignificant to Naaman. He realized that he could not trust in his own power and position, but instead needed to believe in the power of God. The works of God can bring the proudest man to a state of humility. As Christians, we must realize that walking on the red carpet is not as important as walking in the footsteps of Jesus.

Bible Study Questions

1. What was the stigma in Naaman's life? (II Kings 5:1, KJV)

2. Who did God use to tell Naaman about Prophet Elisha? (II Kings 5:2-3, KJV)
3. What did Naaman expect when he arrived at Elisha's house? (II Kings 5:11, KJV)
4. Who did God use to convince Naaman to follow Elisha's instructions? (II Kings 5:13, KJV)
5. Are you more receptive to advice from people you consider to be highly educated and prominent? (Personal Reflection)

Topic: Don't Allow the Past to Block Your Present Blessings
(Was not this the carpenter's son?)
Scripture Reference: Matthew 13:53-58

Insight: It is always easier for us to dismiss our own past than the past of others.

It is in our human nature to doubt a person's present accomplishments when we are familiar with what we perceive to be their past flaws. The people in Jesus' hometown had watched him play as a child and were not willing to accept his power as the Savior. They were willing to accept a misleading family history and could not recognize the Redeemer.

"And they were offended in him. But Jesus said unto them, A prophet is not without honour, save in his own country, and in his own house" Matthew 13:57 (KJV).

The circumstances surrounding Jesus' birth, or at least what they perceived to be the true circumstances about his birth, were well known by the people in his hometown. They knew him as the son of Mary but questioned the paternity of his father. They knew his siblings and Joseph the carpenter, who had assumed the role of his father.

After all, they had watched as he grew up with the other children and they had not received an invitation to his graduation from the seminary. And then there he was, back in town, teaching with such wisdom and authority. It was too amazing to be true. They could not get further than the past and they could not move beyond their astonishment.

If someone from another town had come to Jesus' hometown and began teaching in the synagogue, he would have had a much better chance of being accepted. No one would know about this person's past, and of course, he could show them his credentials, whether genuine or fake. Because the only knowledge that they would have of this individual would be present knowledge, he would have been readily accepted.

Jesus, being all knowing, had not expected to see the welcome wagon rolling down the streets of Nazareth. Unfortunately, the majority of the people could not recognize him as Savior and Lord. There were some, however, who did believe and were healed and made whole. "And he did not many mighty works there because of their unbelief" Matthew 13:58 (KJV).

When a change takes place in your life and you become a Christian who has a personal relationship with Jesus, it is often difficult for family members and friends to accept that change. If they do not know the Jesus you know, it is difficult for them to believe that Jesus is now the center of your life. Many will say, "I knew you when…" And that is your chance to seize the opportunity to let them know who you are now. If they are still living in that sinful past that God snatched you out of, here is your present podium where you can proclaim the good news of the Gospel.

Acknowledge that, yes, you did all those things that they remember, but then let them know that you are so thankful that God allowed you to live long enough to be delivered from that past. Tell them that you are also thankful that God has allowed them to live long enough to witness the change in you and that God is able to deliver them also if they will only surrender their lives to Christ.

Jesus was willing to return to his hometown and be subjected to the old rumors from the past about his birth. He was willing to face the rejection of nonbelievers. He could have easily gone to the next town and been welcomed with open arms. But that was the easy way out. Facing difficult situations to lead people to Christ is what Christianity is all about. Your message will not always be popular, but if one person receives it and is led to Christ, then the sacrifice is not in vain. Jesus knew the hearts of the people, and he also knew who would be receptive to his words and those who would reject them. "My sheep hear my voice, and I know them, and they follow me: And I give unto them eternal life; and they shall never perish, neither shall any man pluck them out of my hand" John 10:27-28.

Be careful when you judge people by their past. Your blessing might be in the message they are delivering in the present.

Bible Study Questions

1. What did Jesus do when he returned to his own country? (Matthew 13:54, KJV)
2. What questions did the people ask about Jesus' family history? (Matthew 13:55-56, KJV)
3. Was Jesus surprised at the reception he received in Nazareth? (Matthew 13:57, KJV)
4. Did Jesus do any mighty works in his hometown? (Mark 6:5-6, KJV)
5. When you became a Christian with a testimony, did you encounter any rejection from your former acquaintances? (Personal Reflection)

Chapter 13: Don't Leave Preparation on the Pew

Topic: Missing the Midnight Madness Sale

(Five foolish virgins with empty lamps)

Scripture Reference: Matthew 25:1-13

Insight: Abraham Lincoln once said, "If I had six hours to chop down a tree, I'd spend the first hour sharpening the ax." This quote says a lot about preparation.

Although there have been at least 242 predicted dates documenting the end of the world, no one knows when the world will end. However, that should not keep us from trying to be prepared for the coming of Christ.

"And while they went to buy, the bridegroom came; and they that were ready went in with him to the marriage: and the door was shut. Afterward came also the other virgins, saying, Lord, Lord, open to us. But he answered and said, Verily I say unto you, I know you not. Watch therefore, for ye know neither the day nor the hour wherein the Son of man cometh" Matthew 25:10-13 (KJV).

Imagine the following scenario, and if you have been blessed with children, the very thought of something like this happening will break your heart. Your eight-year-old is about to go on his first overnight field trip and he is so excited that he cannot keep still. He has everything packed, and the only thing left to do is prepare his backpack with food. As you begin to pack, you notice that there are several items you forgot to purchase. You assure him that you will stop at the store on the way to the meeting spot. He keeps saying that he does not want to miss the bus and you assure him that he will not. The bus is scheduled to leave at 9:00 am, and you are certain that you have plenty of time to spare.

You load up the car and discover that your gas tank is nearly on empty. You know that you do not have enough gas to make it to the location, so you stop for gas. Well, the card reader at the pump is not working, so the two of you go inside so that you can pay for the gas. Your next stop is at the grocery store. He quickly chooses his snacks and the two of you rush toward the front of the store. You hurry to the express lane, only to discover that it is not open. There is only one lane open and you are behind a lady who is buying thirty cans of cat food while arguing with the cashier about the price.

At this point, you know that you will not make it there on time, but surely, they will hold the bus since they know you are on your way. After spending twenty minutes in the grocery store and listening to your son complain that he is going to be late, the two of you finally make it to the car. Although you speed all the way to the pick-up point, to your disappointment, you discover that the bus has already gone. A few of the parents are still there and they explain that the leader of the group said that they could not disappoint the students and they had to leave on time. If only you had stopped for gas the night before. If only you had purchased the necessary items ahead of time. You have so much love and compassion for your child that it hurts you to see that look of disappointment on his face because he missed the bus—because you were not prepared.

These five foolish virgins were not prepared for the bridegroom's arrival. They were half prepared. They had their lamps but had not bothered to bring along extra oil. They just grabbed their lamps and out the door they went. The bridegroom took longer to come than they expected, so they fell asleep. When the bridegroom arrived, the wise virgins trimmed their lamps but the foolish virgins did not have any oil.

They asked the wise virgins for oil, but the wise virgins stood steadfast and were not about to be moved by their pleas. They told them that they (the wise virgins) were not going to risk running out of oil, and that was the reason they came prepared. They instructed the foolish virgins to go and buy oil for their lamps.

Wouldn't you know it? When the foolish virgins got to the store, they discovered only one register open. By the time they returned, the door was locked and the bridegroom would not let them in. They came lacking oil and now they were locked out. "But he answered and said, Verily I say unto you, I know you not. Watch therefore, for ye know neither the day nor the hour wherein the Son of man cometh" Matthew 25:12-13.

There is no doubt that Jesus will return, but we do not know when. It is imperative that we live our lives in conjunction with the Word of God. Not only do we not know when Jesus will return, but we do not know how long it will be before our lives come to an end. If you are a born-again Christian and have a personal relationship with Jesus, then your number one priority is to look forward to his coming and to do everything that you can to help lead others to him.

We will not have time to run out and try and get saved. There will be no express lane that you can go through to get to Heaven. We have to be watchful and stay in God's Word so that we will not be on the outside of a closed door or arriving too late to board the bus.

Bible Study Questions

1. Why were five of the virgins referred to as foolish? (Matthew 25:2-3, KJV)
2. What did the virgins do while they waited for the bridegroom's arrival? (Matthew 25:5, KJV)
3. How was the bridegroom's arrival announced? (Matthew 25:6, KJV)
4. What consequences did the foolish virgins encounter? (Matthew 25:7-9, KJV)

5. How did the bridegroom respond when the late foolish virgins wanted to enter the door? (Matthew 25:10-12, KJV)

Topic: Sometimes You Just Gotta Do What You Gotta Do
Scripture Reference: Acts 5:12-42

Insight: Where spreading the Gospel is concerned, we should always follow God's command.

When a person is in an unfortunate situation, the contributing factor can sometimes be traced to a decision made by that individual. Prior to the pronouncement of the resolution to the problem, the person will say, "If I get out of this, I won't ever do that again." In many cases, when they do get out of the situation, they may stick to the declaration and not repeat the mistake, or they may do just the opposite and even elevate the problem.

Peter and the apostles found themselves in a situation that, on face value, appeared to be an unfortunate one. However, disobedience to God was not an option. The Scripture tells us that Peter and the apostles were performing signs and wonders among the people. "There came also a multitude out of the cities round about unto Jerusalem, bringing sick folks, and them which were vexed with unclean spirits: and they were healed every one. Then the high priest rose up, and all they that were with him, (which is the sect of the Sadducees,) and were filled with indignation, And laid their hands on the apostles, and put them in the common prison" Acts 5:16-18.

The signs and wonders that were being performed by Peter and the apostles caused great multitudes of people to believe in the Lord. "And by the hands of the apostles were many signs and wonders wrought among the people; (and they were all with one accord in Solomon's porch. And of the rest durst no man join himself to them: but the people magnified them. And believers were the more added to the Lord, multitudes both of men and women.)" Acts 5:12-14. There was great enthusiasm and a strong desire to be near this move of God. People started to come from cities around Jerusalem, bringing their sick and demonic possessed to be healed.

The high priest and his followers resented the way the people responded to Peter and the apostles. Their solution was to arrest Peter and the apostles and throw them into prison. They would later discover that this decision was not a wise one.

The officers found themselves in a situation similar to that of the jailer who thought Paul and Silas were securely locked in jail. The guards posted outside the tomb of Jesus could also take part in this conversation because they thought the stone placed outside Jesus' tomb would keep his body safely inside.

The prison was shut and the keepers were standing outside, but when the officers entered, Peter and the apostles were not there. The Scripture states that an angel came in the night. "But the angel of the

Lord by night opened the prison doors, and brought them forth, and said, Go, stand and speak in the temple to the people all the words of this life" Acts 5:19-20 (KJV).

Peter and the apostles did exactly as the angel instructed and returned to the temple to speak God's word. Once the officers returned Peter and the apostles to the prison, they questioned them as to why they went right back to speaking in the temple after they were commanded not to. Peter and the apostles had to let them know that they had a commission to fulfill. "Then Peter and the other apostles answered and said, We ought to obey God rather than men" Acts 5:29 (KJV).

There is a difference in a person being used by God and God using the actions of someone. Just as the envy and jealousy of Joseph's brothers resulted in greater blessings for Joseph, so did the grand speech that Gamaliel delivered before the council resulted in blessings for Peter and the apostles. Gamaliel convinced the council that they had seen leaders in the past who were able to garner great crowds, but that ultimately, the movements came to nothing, and that was the reason why they should release these men and the result would probably be the same. Gamaliel also let them know that if it were truly of God, then they could not win the fight. Gamaliel did not realize that this movement was like none other, and it would not fizzle because it indeed came from God.

After the council had the apostles beaten, they released them and once again commanded them to not speak in the name of Jesus. And the apostles rejoiced because they had been counted worthy to suffer for Jesus' name. What did they do next? You guessed it, they went right back and began to speak about Christ. "And daily in the temple, and in every house, they ceased not to teach and preach Jesus Christ" Acts 5:42 (KJV). Sometimes, you just gotta do what you gotta do.

Bible Study Questions

1. What happened when an attempt was made to stop the apostles from healing the sick? (Acts 5:12-14, KJV)
2. What were the people who were sick and demon possessed doing to reach Peter and the apostles? (Acts 5:15-16, KJV)
3. How did the Sadducees react to Peter and the apostles healing the sick? (Acts 5:17-18, KJV)
4. What teaching assignment did the angel bring from the Lord? (Acts 5:20, KJV)
5. After being placed back into prison and beaten, how did Peter and the apostles react to the demand that they stopped teaching God's word? (Acts 5:27-32, KJV)

Topic: Do I Have Your Attention Now?

(God used Balaam's donkey to get his attention)

Scripture Reference: Numbers 22:5-35

Insight: The voices in your head may be too noisy to hear God's still, small voice.

"And the LORD opened the mouth of the ass, and she said unto Balaam, What have I done unto thee, that thou hast smitten me these three times?" Numbers 22:28 (KJV).

In all his superiority to animals, man is still nothing without God. God can use whatever He chooses to fulfill His purposes.

Balak feared the children of Israel, knowing what they had done to the Amorites, so he sent his princes to Balaam, requesting that he come to him and curse the children of Israel so that he would be able to defeat them. God told Balaam not to go with the men and not to curse the people because they were blessed people.

Balaam refused to go with them and sent back the message to Balak. Balak then sent higher-ranking princes and a message to Balaam that he could have whatever he desired if he would only come. "And Balaam answered and said unto the servants of Balak, If Balak would give me his house full of silver and gold, I cannot go beyond the word of the LORD my God, to do less or more" Numbers 22:18. After this second request from Balak, God instructed Balaam that he was to go with the men but that God would tell him what he should do.

God let Balaam know that there would be further instructions that he would need to follow. "And God came unto Balaam at night, and said unto him, If the men come to call thee, rise up, and go with them; but yet the word which I shall say unto thee, that shalt thou do" Numbers 22:20. The statement "but yet the word which I shall say unto thee, that shalt thou do" should have been an indication to Balaam that the Lord had more instructions for him so that he would not just be riding off blindly with these princes of Balak.

However, that was exactly what Balaam did. "And Balaam rose up in the morning, and saddled his ass, and went with the princes of Moab" Numbers 22:21. Since Balaam had not waited for further instructions, God's anger was kindled and the angel of the Lord stood in the way as an adversary against him. Balaam did not see the angel standing in the way with his sword drawn, but the donkey that he was riding on saw the angel and ran off into the field. Balaam struck the donkey and turned her back onto the road.

The Bible says, "But the angel of the LORD stood in a path of the vineyards, a wall being on this side, and a wall on that side" Numbers 22:24 (KJV). Once again, Balaam did not see the angel, but the donkey did. So the donkey thrust herself into the wall and crushed Balaam's foot against it, and Balaam struck the donkey again.

After Balaam's actions, the angel of the Lord went further, and stood in a narrow place where Balaam was trapped with no way out. The donkey once again saw the angel of the Lord, so she just fell down. Balaam was really upset now. The Bible says "he smote the ass with a staff."

At this point, the Lord allowed the donkey to give her testimony. “And the LORD opened the mouth of the ass, and she said unto Balaam, What have I done unto thee, that thou hast smitten me these three times?” Numbers 22:28 (KJV).

“And the ass said unto Balaam, Am not I thine ass, upon which thou hast ridden ever since I was thine unto this day? was I ever wont to do so unto thee? and he said, Nay” Numbers 22:30 (KJV). Then the Lord opened Balaam’s eyes so that he could see what the donkey had been seeing all along.

The angel of the Lord wanted to know why Balaam had struck the donkey three times. If it had not been for the donkey, Balaam would have been killed by the angel of the Lord.

Balaam acknowledged that he had sinned and wanted to turn around on his journey. The angel of the Lord told him that he should continue on, but only speak the words that he would give him to speak.

God used Balaam’s donkey to keep him alive. God’s choices of faith instruments may seem strange to us. He had to give the donkey the voice of reason in this situation. How often do we try and do things on our own without seeking and waiting for direction from God? “Trust in the LORD with all thine heart; and lean not unto thine own understanding. In all thy ways acknowledge him, and he shall direct thy paths” Proverbs 3:5-6 (KJV).

Bible Study Questions

1. Why did Balak fear the children of Israel? (Numbers 22:3, KJV)
2. Why did Balaam refuse to curse the children of Israel? (Numbers 22:12, KJV)
3. How many times did the ass try to warn Balaam? (Numbers 22:28, KJV)
4. What were the angel's words to Balaam? (Numbers 22:32-33, KJV)
5. Is it hard for God to get your attention? (Personal Reflection)

Topic: God Has Already Crossed the State Line
(David expressed the omnipresence of God)
Scripture Reference: Psalm 139:7-24

Insight: God is only as far away from us as we allow ourselves to be distanced from Him.

"Whither shall I go from thy spirit? or whither shall I flee from thy presence?" Psalm 139:7 (KJV).

It is not difficult to find God; He is everywhere. He transcends borders and boundaries. Circumstances in life sometimes dictate that we make major changes. Relocating to another part of the country is sometimes one of the changes that we face. We must realize that no matter where we go, God is already there.

In verses 8 through 12 of Psalm 139, David described God's all-knowing power. David felt that this was beyond his human comprehension. "If I ascend up into heaven, thou art there: if I make my bed in hell, behold, thou art there. If I take the wings of the morning, and dwell in the uttermost parts of the sea; Even there shall thy hand lead me, and thy right hand shall hold me. If I say, Surely the darkness shall cover me; even the night shall be light about me. Yea, the darkness hideth not from thee; but the night shineth as the day: the darkness and the light are both alike to thee."

There is no place that you can go where God is not already there. There is no thought that you can think that God does not already know. When David expressed his thoughts concerning God's omniscience, he could not help but refer to Him also as being omnipresent. David realized that God knew his every move and there was no escaping from His presence.

So why is it that when we move to new locations, we decide not to include God in the trip? Students going away to college who have participated in youth activities in church, given welcome addresses, sang in the choir, and served on the youth usher board seem to think that college is no place for God.

Why is it that individuals leaving small towns who grew up going to church every day except Saturday, whose lives revolved around what was going on at the local church, feel that God can't make the trip across the state line to the big city?

The answer is simple: they were a member of a church but had not developed a personal relationship with the Father. Once you know that Jesus is your personal Savior, there will be no doubt that wherever you go, He is already there. Whatever venture you pursue, Jesus is a step ahead of you. If He was Jesus when you were in Sunday school, he will be Jesus at Harvard or Princeton. If he was Jesus in Rural County, USA, he will be Jesus in New York City or Dallas, Texas.

The determining factor is whether he was really in your heart in Sunday school or he was really in your heart in the small town that you came from. God does not change, but we do.

Have you ever gotten off an airplane and saw people holding up signs with the names of arriving passengers? In most cases, they are not sure who they are there to pick up, and the person being picked up has no idea who is there to transport him to his destination. No matter what bus, plane, or train you step out of, the same two greeters will be at every bus terminal, airport, and train station. One is Jesus and the other is Satan. Now, if you doubt that Jesus will be there, it is more than likely that Satan helped you pack your bags, was there when your ticket was stamped, and actually walked off the bus, plane, or train at the same time you did.

If you have a personal relationship with Jesus, although Satan is there holding up a sign, beckoning you to look in his direction, you will walk right past him and into the loving arms of Jesus, who will be there to lead, guide, and protect you just as he did prior to your crossing the state line. You do not have to carry him across the state line; he will be there when you arrive.

We have to learn how to listen for his voice only. "My sheep hear my voice, and I know them, and they follow me: And I give unto them eternal life; and they shall never perish, neither shall any man pluck them out of my hand" John 10:27-28.

Bible Study Questions

1. Where could David go to escape from God? (Psalm 139:7-12, KJV)
2. How did David describe the omniscience of God? (Psalm 139:1-4, KJV)
3. As Christians, how can we determine if God is speaking to us through preachers? (I John 4:1-4, KJV)
4. Have you ever relocated and felt like you left God behind? (Personal Reflection)
5. Does God really and truly have first place in your heart? (Personal Reflection)

www.ingramcontent.com/pod-product-compliance
Lightning Source LLC
LaVergne TN
LVHW010058110826
845155LV00028B/393
9781936746675